SCHOLASTIC

Vocabulary Activities
Just for Young Learners

Pamela Chanko

D1455939

NEW YORK • TORONTO • LONDON • AUCKLAND • SYDNEY

MEXICO CITY • NEW DELHI • HONG KONG • BUENOS AIRES

Teaching *Resources*

For Abby,
the vocabulary virtuoso
who is (almost) always right.

The following activities were adapted from *Teaching With Favorite Mem Fox Books* by Pamela Chanko (Scholastic, 2005): "Feelings and Faces Book;" "Snack-Time Stories;" "Animal Tracks Accordion Book;" "Lost and Found."

Editor: Joan Novelli
Cover design: Brian LaRossa
Cover photograph © gettyimages.com/OJO Images.
Interior design: Kathy Massaro
Interior art: James Graham Hale

ISBN-13: 978-0-545-04592-6
ISBN-10: 0-545-04592-4
Copyright © 2009 by Pamela Chanko.
Illustrations © 2009 by Scholastic Inc.
All rights reserved.
Printed in the U.S.A.

1 2 3 4 5 6 7 8 9 10   31   15 14 13 12 11 10 09

Contents

Theme Units

Introduction

What does it mean to have a strong vocabulary? The answer to this question is severalfold. Having a strong vocabulary means you get more out of what you read, because you comprehend it on a deeper level. Having a strong vocabulary means you are a better writer, because you have the words you need to express exactly what you want to. Having a strong vocabulary means you have the capacity to study and learn in a variety of subject areas, because words are the tools for understanding new concepts. Having a strong vocabulary means you have improved social skills, because you are able to articulate your own thoughts and understand the thoughts of others. In short, having a strong vocabulary opens all the doors.

Research shows that direct instruction is essential to vocabulary building, and that learning new words requires multiple encounters and repeated instruction. But memorizing words and their definitions is unlikely to engage children, and it is of paramount importance that children not only learn words, but also learn to be interested in words. That's where this book comes in! *Vocabulary Activities Just for Young Learners* features a wealth of activities that invite children to engage in the *fun* of exploring words. Here are just a few examples of the types of hands-on, interactive activities you'll find in these pages:

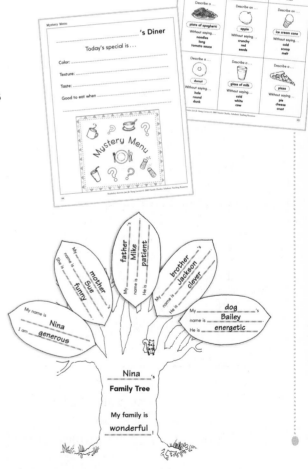

✳ collaborative books

✳ board games and card games

✳ piggyback versions of favorite children's tunes

✳ interactive bulletin board displays

✳ physical activities for kinesthetic learners

✳ word puzzles

✳ and more!

This book is designed to fit right in with your existing curriculum. It's flexible, so you can choose activities that correspond with the themes you already teach, such as weather and seasons, families, animals, transportation, and the five senses. Engaging children actively with vocabulary helps develop a love of language that can last a lifetime—so get ready to welcome children into the wonderful world of words!

How to Use This Book

The activities and lessons in this book are designed to provide you with hands-on ideas and materials that will help you put the latest research into action in your classroom all year long. Following is a list of the features you'll find.

✳ **Research Base** (Pages 6–8): Use the information on these pages to familiarize yourself with the theoretical framework on which the activities and lessons are based. Review guidelines for choosing words to teach (including developmentally appropriate vocabulary) and suggestions for direct and indirect instruction.

✳ **Everyday Vocabulary Building** (Pages 8–10): From how to make the most of transition times to quick and easy ways of using word walls, these tips offer simple solutions for building vocabulary-learning into your busy classroom schedule.

✳ **Assessment Strategies** (Pages 10–12): The assessment suggestions here are designed to track children's progress. Both verbal activities and a sample rubric are included to assist you in formal and informal assessments.

✳ **Meeting the Standards** (Page 12): The activities in this book support a range of language arts skills, listed on this page.

✳ **Theme Units and Reproducible Activity Pages** (Pages 13–80): Each theme unit is based on a popular primary teaching theme, so you'll be able to fit direct vocabulary instruction into your existing curriculum. The lessons are organized for flexibility; you can complete them in any order. A synopsis of each theme unit appears at the beginning of each unit, making it easy to match activities to your students' interests and needs. Step-by-step directions guide you through each activity.

Activities for each theme unit include at least one reproducible activity page, putting ready-to-use board games, collaborative book templates, bulletin-board display patterns, and more right at your fingertips!

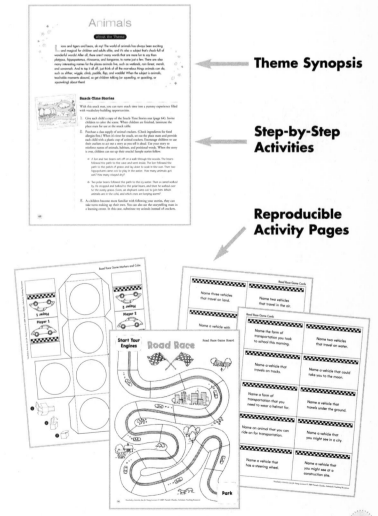

Theme Synopsis

Step-by-Step Activities

Reproducible Activity Pages

Why Teach Vocabulary? What the Research Says

As a teacher of young children, you have probably noticed that students come to school with a wide range of vocabulary knowledge. Some seem to own knowledge of a great deal of words, while others have far fewer in their repertoire. This can be the result of a multitude of factors, but what's most important to note is that children who are farther behind on this continuum tend to *stay* behind unless they have direct instruction. When wide independent reading is counted on to build vocabulary, these students are often at a disadvantage. Why? Because struggling readers simply don't read well enough to utilize this channel of learning (Beck, McKeown, and Kucan, 2002).

Research has clearly shown that increased vocabulary relates directly to overall comprehension and reading success. However, improved ability in the area of language arts is just one of many benefits. A good working vocabulary is necessary in order for children to learn concepts in science, social studies, and math, and also leads to improved social skills. In short, words help children acquire knowledge by enabling them to understand and express what they experience in their environment, whether in school, at home, or in texts (Blachowicz, Fisher, and Watts-Taffe, 2005).

Fluency and Word Knowledge

Fluency is the ability to read text accurately, smoothly, and quickly, with appropriate expression when reading aloud. Said to be the bridge to comprehension, fluency allows readers to focus their attention on getting meaning rather than on decoding. While word recognition is one of the keys to fluency, a child may be able to recognize, read, and pronounce a word but still not know its meaning (Blachowicz et al., 2005). Therefore, deep word knowledge is critical to achieving ongoing fluency and reading success.

Children can "pick up" some new words from reading. However, not all children are accomplished enough readers to do this. A second problem with relying on written context is that the context is limited. Authors make word choices in the service of their stories, not in order to teach vocabulary, and so these context definitions can be misleading. For instance, a story may describe a character as "facing the bright, beautiful new day with *dread*," which could lead a reader to believe that *dread* is a kind of optimism—when in fact, a character who was hoping it would rain would feel quite the opposite! It's also important to remember that learning a new word involves multiple, repeated encounters with the word in a variety of contexts. If a child encounters the word *dread* in a single text, who's to say when the next encounter will take place? And finally, written text does not involve several factors that help children learn words, such as body language, tone of voice, and personal experience within a situation (Beck et al., 2002). Therefore, there is a tremendous need for direct and focused vocabulary instruction in the classroom.

Choosing Words to Teach

There are far too many words in our language to be able to address each one directly. What makes direct vocabulary instruction possible is the fact that not all words require it. The most basic words, such as *happy, walk,* and *cat,* usually do not need to be taught. Beck, McKeown, and Kucan refer to these as "Tier One" words (2002). Words that are considered "Tier Three" words, such as *longitude* and *chlorophyll,* are rarely used outside of academic contexts, and it is usually best to learn these words as they come up in a particular course of study. The words that teachers need to focus on, then, when providing direct vocabulary instruction, are what Beck and her colleagues call "Tier Two" words. These words, such as *ridiculous, persevere, enormous,* and *ferocious,* are used often in mature language, and are useful in a variety of contexts, but are not so simple that children already know them well (Beck et al., 2002). When choosing words to teach, keep in mind their general usefulness, as well as the level of your students.

What words are developmentally appropriate to teach at each level? There is no scientific formula to answer this question, and we can't rely on grade-level word lists to tell us. If a particular word is classified as a "fourth-grade word," this only means that most children don't know the word before fourth grade—not that they aren't *capable* of learning the word before fourth grade. Any word can be on-level for any student, as long as it has two features: first, you should be able to define the target word using words that children already know. If the only words that can be used to explain the target word are also unknown to children, the word is too difficult. The second criterion is the word's usefulness in everyday life and its capacity to express common concepts in a sophisticated and mature manner. Beck and her colleagues state that "kindergartners readily applied *nuisance* to disruptive classmates, and understood what was happening when a *commotion* occurred in the hall; first graders could easily discern *argumentative* peers from those who acted *dignified*!" (Beck et al., 2002, p. 29).

Making Words Come Alive

All of us probably remember the vocabulary exercise we were asked to do most often in school: in order to practice a new word, we were told to look it up in the dictionary and then use it in a sentence. The first problem with this type of work is that dictionary definitions are limited and can be misleading. The second problem is that it's incredibly boring! There are two essential factors involved in the effective instruction of vocabulary. The first is, of course, teaching the words themselves. The second is just as important: Teaching children to *love words*. The more fun children have with words inside the classroom, the more they are likely to pay attention to them outside the classroom, in every situation they experience. People with great vocabularies can almost always be characterized as being fascinated with words and their meanings (Beck et al., 2002). We need to develop children's curiosity about the meanings of words, and how words relate to one another.

Showing children that words and language can be interesting and fun is the key to successful vocabulary development.

Research shows that the best way to help children expand their vocabularies is through a combination of direct and indirect instruction (Armbruster and Osborn, 2001; National Institute of Child Health and Human Development, 2000). In direct instruction, children learn words through school-based activities and lessons. In indirect instruction, children learn words by seeing and hearing them in different situations, such as conversations with adults and literature that is read aloud.

Everyday Vocabulary Building

Research clearly shows that in order to build a strong vocabulary, children not only need to be surrounded by words, they also need to *actively engage* with words on an everyday basis. Following are some general tips and activities for creating a vocabulary-rich environment that invites interaction.

* **Word Associations:** Make the most out of transition times by using them to build word associations. In advance, create pairs of index cards with words that go together. Use a more commonly known word with a more sophisticated word to make a matching pair. For instance, if you're learning weather words, you might pair *hot* with *broiling*. If you're focusing on words that describe feelings, you might pair *sad* with *gloomy*. Make sure that each card will have only one match, and keep the cards in a paper bag. Whenever you're doing an activity that requires partners (such as transitioning to a curriculum project, or even just lining up two-by-two to leave the classroom), have each child reach into the bag and pick a random card. Children pair up by looking for the classmate who has the word that makes a match with their own.

* **Word Walls:** Several of the activities in this book involve the creation of word walls. (Note that every classroom can have a few different word walls up at the same time.) As long as new words are introduced gradually (so that children aren't overwhelmed with a barrage of new vocabulary at once), word walls can be a constant source of interaction throughout each school day. For instance, you can have each child guess a "mystery word" from a word wall before selecting a center for choice time (simply give definition and/or spelling clues). Or, choose a word from the wall to be the "secret password" for entering the classroom (children must use the word in a sentence before coming in).

* **Teachable Moments:** Be sure to expose children to sophisticated language in everyday situations. Be alert and take advantage of opportunities to introduce "grown-up" words in conversation. For instance, if a child is working very hard at a task, you might comment on her *concentration*. If a child produces a particularly well-done piece of work, you might say it's *remarkable*. Children may wonder what the new word means, and this can result in a meaningful discussion in which

children have the opportunity to experience the word in a context that relates to them. Again, it's important not to overwhelm children with a constant stream of new vocabulary; you can be spontaneous, but also use judgment when "sprinkling" your conversations with new words.

* **Scavenger Hunts:** Children need to encounter sophisticated vocabulary both inside and outside of school, so that they can see how words are used in a variety of contexts and situations. One way to help children pay attention to words is to encourage scavenger hunting. Set up a "Word Detective" bulletin board or wall in the classroom by writing each student's name at the top of a sheet of posterboard and keeping a supply of sticky notes nearby. Each week, you can give children a few target words to "catch red-handed"—that is, see, hear, or read in action outside of school. Children might hear the word on television or the radio, see it in their independent reading, or even use it themselves in a conversation at home. After reporting on how the word was used, children write the word on a sticky note and attach it to their poster. You can establish goals for children by giving them special certificates once they've accumulated a predetermined number of sticky notes on their poster.

* **Read-Aloud Literature:** As young children are still learning to be fluent readers, most books targeted for their reading level are not good sources for building vocabulary. Children's speaking and listening vocabulary develops much sooner than their reading vocabulary, so it's important to engage children in texts that they may not be able to read on their own, but are capable of understanding when read aloud. It's helpful to discuss any unfamiliar words during and after your reading, because the story can give children a good context for understanding. It's also a good idea to use the new words in situations outside the story, over an extended period of time. For example, after reading Maurice Sendak's *Where the Wild Things Are* (in which Max, the main character, starts a wild rumpus), you can ask, "What's all the *rumpus* about?" the next time the classroom gets too noisy!

* **Dictionary Do's and Don'ts:** While dictionaries do provide brief introductions to words, keep in mind that these references are limited because of the nature of the format; the definitions not only need to be concise but also often use academic rather than "everyday" language. Children should be familiar with dictionaries and know how to use them in their independent learning. But often, the best way to meaningfully introduce a new word is by defining it yourself in child-friendly terms. Be as specific as possible and discuss common situations in which the word would be appropriately applied. For instance, a dictionary definition for the word *admit* is *to confess to something, or agree that something is true, often reluctantly.* The words *confess* and *reluctantly* would make this definition unhelpful to most children. However, children are much more likely to understand the meaning

Bibliography

Armbruster, B. B., and Osborn, M. (2001). *Put reading first: The research building blocks for teaching children to read, kindergarten through grade 3.* Washington, DC: Center for the Improvement of Early Reading Achievement (CIERA).

Beck, I. L., McKeown, M. G., and Kucan, L. (2002). *Bringing words to life: robust vocabulary instruction.* New York, NY: Guilford Press.

Blachowicz, C. L. Z., Fisher, P. J., and Watts-Taffe, S. (2005). *Integrated vocabulary instruction: Meeting the needs of diverse learners in grades K—5.* Naperville, IL: Learning Point Associates.

Block, C. C. and Mangieri, J. N. (2004). *Powerful vocabulary for reading success.* New York, NY: Scholastic.

National Institute of Child Health and Human Development, NIH, DHHS. (2000). *Report of the National Reading Panel: Teaching children to read: Reports of the subgroups (00-4754).* Washington, DC: U.S. Government Printing Office.

with an explanation such as, *When you* admit *to something, it means you're telling the truth, even when part of you doesn't want to. You might not want to tell people that you made a mistake, but in the end, you have to tell the truth. So if your brother can't find his favorite book and asks you what happened to it, you might* admit *that you lost it.*

✳ **Word Play:** Create an atmosphere that emphasizes the fun that children can have with words. You can introduce children to crosswords, which provide a fun way to think about a word's definition. You might create your own Pictionary-style game by writing target words on index cards, having children choose a word at random, and challenging them to draw a picture that will help their classmates guess the word. Word Bingo is also a fun option: Simply have children write target words on a grid in random order, and then call out definitions. When children hear the definition for a word on their board, they can cover it with a marker. In addition, words written on index cards are a great resource for card games. For instance, children can play a version of "Go Fish" by trying to acquire synonym pairs, or they can play "Concentration" to match up antonyms, synonyms, or words and their definitions.

✳ **Home-School Connections:** Since word power is built both in and out of school, try to involve children's families in students' vocabulary development as much as possible. Invite parents and caregivers into the classroom to observe how you read a story aloud and discuss the vocabulary with children. Send children out the door with take-home packs, including both a book and a quick vocabulary-building activity for after reading, such as coming up with five words to describe a character or inventing a new line of dialogue using a target word from the book. Keep families informed about the words children are learning at school and give them ideas for word games they can play during daily activities. For instance, families might look for target food-related words while grocery shopping, or play verbal word games such as 20 Questions or I Spy while traveling in the car.

Assessment Strategies

As children's vocabulary increases, you'll want to track their expanding word-knowledge base. Informal assessment, such as observing children's use of new vocabulary in conversation and tracking their growing interest in words and their meanings, is quite valuable, but more formal assessment will likely give you a clearer picture of where children are in their development. Remember, however, that speaking and listening vocabulary develops along a continuum. There are many different degrees of "knowing" a word, as Isabel Beck and her colleagues note in their book *Bringing Words to Life: Robust Vocabulary Instruction* (2002). The chart at right shows the common stages of acquiring a new word.

Because of this continuum of knowledge, concrete assessments such as multiple-choice vocabulary tests can be limited in their usefulness. These kinds of quizzes do provide some useful information, but they need to be part of a larger picture. As an example, a child who has Stage 3 knowledge of the word *extraordinary* might know that the word has a positive connotation, and might be able to explain it in one context—for instance, the child knows that when he or she has produced good work, the teacher has called it *extraordinary*. This may be enough for the child to choose the correct answer on a multiple choice quiz; however, when asked to explain or use the word *extraordinary* in a context outside schoolwork, the child may not be able to do so—indicating that the child does not in fact have complete knowledge of the word.

There are many different techniques you can use to assess children's knowledge of words on a deeper level. Suggestions follow.

※ **Make Connections Among Words:** Ask questions that encourage children to make connections among a group of target words. For example, for the words *joyous, discouraged,* and *anxious,* you might ask, "Which word goes with *holiday*?" (*joyous*) "Which word goes with losing a basketball game?" (*discouraged*) Encourage children to explain their choices.

※ **Connect Personal Experiences:** Invite children to explain the meanings of words in the context of personal experiences. To assess children's knowledge of the word *confused,* for example, you might ask: "What was a time when you were confused? What made you feel that way?"

※ **Act It Out:** Acting out a word physically can be a particularly good form of assessment for kinesthetic learners. For instance, you might ask children to show how they would look if they were *strolling* and then show how they would look if they were *scurrying*. The differences in their movements can give you good insight as to how well they know each word.

※ **Provide Choices:** Start with the word and have children choose the appropriate example from two closely related choices. For instance, if you want to see how well children know the word *disappointed,* you might ask: "Which is something that would make you feel *disappointed*—having a birthday, or your best friend forgetting your birthday? Why?"

Stages of Word Knowledge

Stage 1: The child has no knowledge of the word; has never seen or heard it.

Stage 2: The child has heard or seen the word, but does not know what it means.

Stage 3: The child has some knowledge of the word and can relate it to one context or situation, but cannot apply it across a variety of contexts or situations.

Stage 4: The child knows the word well, and can explain it and use it readily across many contexts and situations.

From *Bringing Words to Life: Robust Vocabulary Instruction* by Isabel L. Beck, Margaret G. McKeown, and Linda Kucan. Copyright © 2002 The Guilford Press. Adapted with permission of The Guilford Press.

* **Multiple Contexts:** To assess if children know how to use a word across multiple contexts, encourage them to apply the word to more than one situation. For example, if the target word is *challenging*, you might ask: "What is something you do at school that is challenging? What is something that is challenging to do at the playground?"

* **Contextual Questions:** A good way to gauge the depth of children's word knowledge is to provide them with a situational context and then ask a related question about the situation. For instance, if you want to assess how deeply children understand the word *jealous*, you might say: "When Amanda saw Monique's new shoes, she couldn't help looking down at her own sneakers and feeling jealous of her friend. How do you think Amanda feels about her sneakers? Why?"

Meeting the Standards

The lessons and activities in this book support the following standards for students in grades K–2, outlined by Mid-continent Research for Education and Learning (McREL), an organization that collects and synthesizes national and state K–12 curriculum standards.

Uses the general skills and strategies of the writing process:

- Uses prewriting strategies to plan written work (discusses ideas with peers)
- Uses strategies to draft written work (adds descriptive words)
- Uses strategies to edit and publish written work (incorporates illustrations)
- Evaluates own and others' writing
- Uses strategies to organize written work
- Uses writing and other methods to describe familiar persons, places, objects, or experiences
- Writes in a variety of forms or genres
- Writes for different purposes (to entertain, inform, learn, communicate ideas)

Uses the stylistic and rhetorical aspects of writing:

- Uses descriptive words to convey basic ideas

Uses grammatical and mechanical conventions in written compositions:

- Uses complete sentences in written compositions
- Uses nouns in written compositions (nouns for simple objects, family members, community workers, and categories)
- Uses verbs in written compositions (verbs for a variety of situations, action words)

- Uses adjectives in written compositions (uses descriptive words)
- Uses adverbs in written compositions (uses words that answer *how, when, where,* and *why* questions)

Uses the general skills and strategies of the reading process:

- Uses mental images based on pictures and print to aid in comprehension of text
- Understands level-appropriate sight words and vocabulary (words for persons, places, things, actions)

Uses listening and speaking strategies for different purposes:

- Makes contributions in class and group discussions
- Asks and responds to questions
- Uses level-appropriate vocabulary in speech
- Gives and responds to oral directions

Uses viewing skills and strategies to understand and interpret visual media:

- Understands the main idea or message in visual media (pictures, cartoons)

Kendall, J. S. & Marzano, R. J. (2004). *Content knowledge: A compendium of standards and benchmarks for K–12 education.* Aurora, CO: Mid-continent Research for Education and Learning. Online database: http://www.mcrel.org/standards-benchmarks/

All About Me

Children expand their vocabularies when they learn new, more sophisticated ways to talk about concepts they already know. And what do children know most about? Themselves! Giving children more precise words with which to describe themselves not only builds vocabulary, but also self-esteem. So the next time a child talks about something she can do well, you might describe her ability as *exceptional*. When children talk about being "grown-up," you might introduce the word *mature*. The possibilities are endless, because each child is special—in other words, *singular* and *unique*!

Favorite Things Time-Capsule Book

This quick activity is a great way for children to see how they've grown and changed.

1. Toward the beginning of the year, create a fill-in-the-blank survey for children to fill out, encouraging them to tell about their favorite things. Use cloze sentences such as: *My favorite subject is _____ because _____. My favorite activity is _____ because _____. My favorite snack to have at school is _____ because _____.*

2. Have children complete the sentences, encouraging them to use specific words to tell the reasons for their choices. For instance, a child might write: *My favorite subject is art because I like to see how the colors mix together.*

3. When children's surveys are complete, collect them and bind them into a book. After sharing and discussing the book several times, remove it from your library and store it in a safe place.

4. At the end of the year, have children complete the same survey again. Encourage them to complete the sentences in a way that describes how they feel now. For instance, the child who loved art might have discovered a new interest in dramatic play or math. Another child may now have new or more specific words to describe the same preference. Bind the surveys into a new book and read it aloud. Then compare it to your first book to see how children have changed throughout the year.

Same and Different

With this activity, children make connections between words—and each other!

1. Give each child six blank index cards and have children write their name on one card. Then invite children to write a fact about themselves on each of the remaining cards.

2. Circulate as children write, assisting them in finding specific words for their cards. For instance, rather than writing *I like to play outside*, a child might write *I like to ride my bike*. Rather than writing *I love animals*, a child might write *I think lizards are amazing*.

3. When children are finished, have them hold onto their name cards as you collect all of the descriptive cards and place them in a bag or box. Then create two overlapping yarn circles on the floor (or use hula-hoops) to make a Venn diagram.

4. Invite two volunteers to come up to the diagram and have each child place his or her name card above a circle. One at a time, have children take a card from the bag, read it aloud, and discuss how it relates to them. If the information on the card applies to one child, it is placed in that child's circle. If it applies to both children, it is placed in the overlapping section. If it applies to neither child, it is placed outside the diagram.

5. Continue, inviting different combinations of children up to the diagram to see how they are alike and different!

All About Adverbs!

It's not what you do, it's the way that you do it! This fun activity invites children to describe their bodies' actions.

1. Begin by modeling a few adverbs for children. First, walk across the classroom in your usual manner. Then change your walk to express a certain descriptor; for instance, you might walk *slowly* or *quickly*. Invite children to describe the way you are walking. Explain that there are many interesting ways to describe an action like walking. If someone is trying to keep from getting hurt, he or she might walk *cautiously*. If someone is feeling good about him- or herself, that person might walk *confidently*.

2. Together, brainstorm more adverbs that can be applied to walking, making sure to use each word in context and have children give examples to be sure they understand the meaning. Write the words on a sheet of chart paper and also on small slips of paper.

3. Place the slips of paper in a bag and invite a volunteer to come up and choose one. Have the child walk across the room in the manner described on the slips of paper. It's the group's job to look at the word list and guess which word the child is acting out. Continue until each child has had a chance to act out a word.

All About Me Song

Invite children to create piggyback lyrics as they sing about what makes them unique.

1. Begin by singing the traditional version of *Twinkle, Twinkle, Little Star* with children. Sing the song several times, until children are comfortable with the tune and rhythm.

2. Next, model how to create new lyrics by singing a verse about yourself. Choose a phrase that describes one of your attributes, such as an adjective about your personality, an activity you enjoy, or a favorite food. Then insert the attribute into the song, using the lyrics in the box at right.

3. Invite children each to replace the underlined song words with words about themselves. Repeat the verse to sing a song about each child.

> I'm <u>Ms. Johnson</u>, that's my name,
>
> No one else is quite the same.
>
> <u>I like knitting</u>, don't you see,
>
> No one else is quite like me.
>
> I'm <u>Ms. Johnson</u>, that's my name,
>
> No one else is quite the same.

What's in a Name?

Use children's names as the basis for a variety of vocabulary explorations.

1. If possible, obtain a copy of a baby name book that contains name meanings and origins. Children will be interested to hear their name's "definition," and will likely learn some sophisticated vocabulary in the process. For instance, the name *Jeffrey* means "peaceful land" or "peaceful traveler"; the name *Sophia* means "wisdom"; the name *Austin* means "venerated"; and the name *Alexis* means "defender" or "protector." If children's names are not listed, or they don't think the definition suits them, invite them to come up with the word or phrase they think describes them best!

(continued)

2. Children can use their names to create personalized tongue twisters. Encourage children to write a sentence about themselves, using as many words as they can that begin with the first letter of their first name. For instance, *Hannah is a helpful hero who likes hopscotch, horses, and hamsters!* Each child can write or dictate a tongue twister on a sentence strip, and you can post them on a bulletin board or wall.

Star of the Week

Encourage children to describe themselves and their classmates as each one takes a turn in the spotlight.

1. First, designate wall space or a bulletin board at children's eye level for a rotating "Star of the Week" display. Let children know that each week they will be celebrating a new classmate, and everyone will have a turn.

2. Choose a child at random to be the first week's star. If possible, get a headshot photo and duplicate it so each child has a copy.

3. Discuss attributes that make the week's "star" student unique. Be sure to lead children toward specific language; for instance, if someone says Sara is "nice" ask, "What does Sara do that is nice?" Point out that if Sara shares with everyone, she might be called *generous*; if she is very friendly, she can be described as *outgoing*.

4. Give each child a copy of the reproducible star pattern (page 17; enlarge first, if desired). Have children cut out the star and glue the chosen child's photo in the center circle. (If photos are unavailable, children can draw a portrait of the child.) On the line beneath the picture, have the chosen child write "I am…" and then use the lines on each point to describe him- or herself. Have other students write "[chosen child's name] is…" in this space, and then write words or phrases on each point to describe the featured child.

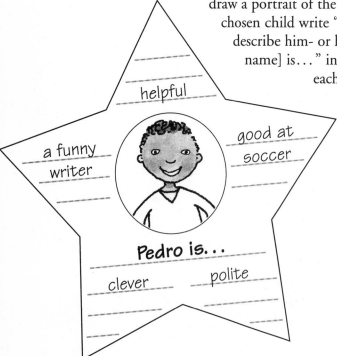

5. Display the completed stars on a bulletin board. You can also post samples of the child's art, writing, or other class work. Discuss the descriptions throughout the week, inviting children to give examples and use the words in sentences. At the end of the week, you can announce the next star-to-be!

Star of the
Week Pattern

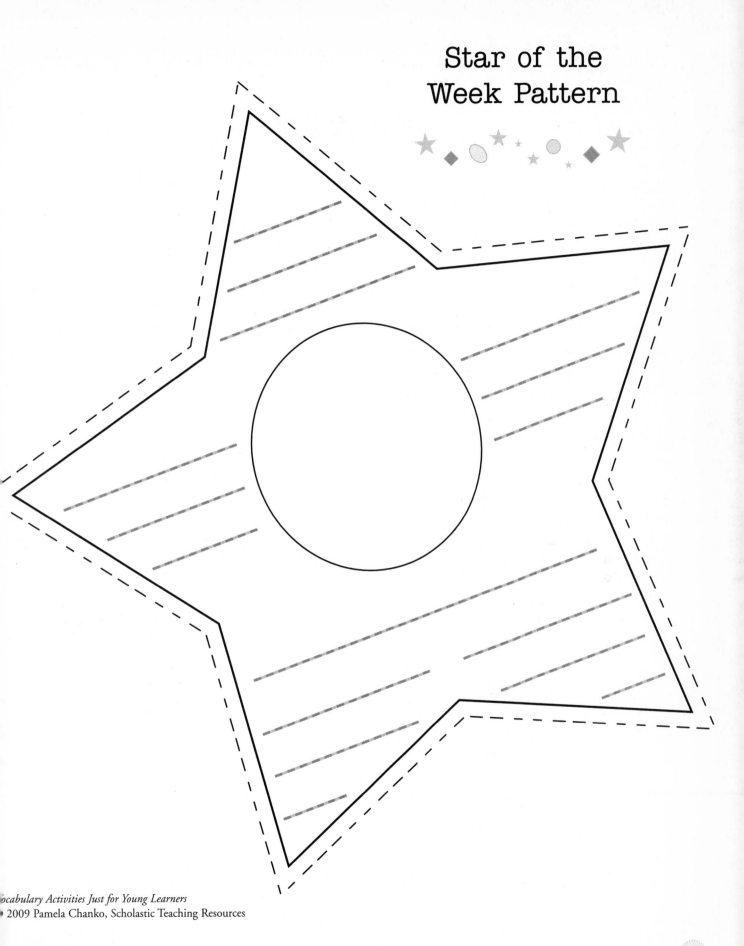

Family and Friends

Fathers, mothers, sisters, brothers, grandparents, friends, classmates, buddies, playmates—we all value family and friends in our lives, and that's why there are so many words to describe them! "Family and Friends" is a great theme for building children's vocabularies, since it's based on their own lives and experiences. In addition, a good vocabulary is the key to effective communication skills—which is what helps us to make connections and build relationships with others. You can increase vocabulary and develop social skills by encouraging children to be specific when they express positive feelings toward their classmates. For instance, rather than simply saying "I like you," in certain circumstances it might be appropriate for a child to say "I admire you" or "I appreciate you." When children describe friends and family members, encourage them to use words that express specific character traits, such as *kindness, generosity, warmth,* or *humor.*

Handy Hellos

Reinforce friendly vocabulary with this "hands-on" activity.

1. To begin, pair children up and give each child a sheet of colored construction paper. Have each child place his or her hand on the paper as the partner traces around it. Then have children cut out their handprints.

2. Next, ask, "What are some things you can say to let someone know you want to be friends?" Brainstorm friendly words and phrases with children, such as *Hello, How do you do?*, *Pleased to meet you,* and so on. Record children's suggestions on the board or chart paper.

3. Next, ask children how they might greet friends. Record their suggestions. You can also include questions for specific situations, such as *Do you want to play? Do you want to share my _____?*

4. Have children choose a greeting from the list, or create one of their own, and write it on their handprint. Then have children sign their names. You can use the handprints to create a friendly word wall, a colorful border for a classroom wall, or you might even glue them to a cardboard circle to make a wreath for your door.

Family Take-Home Journal

Use this activity to build literacy skills along with home-school connections.

1. Choose a story that has a theme related to "families" to send home with children. Possible choices include *A Baby Sister for Frances* by Russell Hoban (Harper, 1964), *The Relatives Came* by Cynthia Rylant (Simon & Schuster, 1985), and *A Chair for My Mother* by Vera B. Williams (William Morrow, 1982).

2. Prepare a fill-in-the-blank response page for children to take home along with the book. Ask vocabulary-building questions in a cloze format, such as those at right. You can also suggest that children draw their favorite scene or character on the back of the page.

> My family enjoyed this book because _____.
>
> Our favorite character was _____ because he/she _____.
>
> We especially liked the scene where _____.

3. Create a take-home pack by placing the book, response page, pencils, and crayons in a zip-close bag. Send the bag home with a different child each night, and have the child return the pack to school the next day. When each child has created a page, make a cover and bind the pages together.

4. Read the book aloud with the class, and then share the collaborative journal. Discuss different families' opinions of the book, and the words they used to express them.

Manners Matter!

Review etiquette with a word-of-the-day calendar!

1. Write the phrase "Polite Words of the Day" across the top of a sheet of posterboard. Label five library card pockets (check local libraries and school supply stores) with a day of the week, from Monday through Friday. Affix the cards to the posterboard. (See sample, page 20.)

2. Next, hold a class discussion on manners. What are some words and phrases children can use to be courteous and polite to others? Brainstorm expressions such as *Excuse me, I'm sorry, Please, Thank you, Pardon me, You're welcome, It's all right,* and *May I.* Write each phrase on an index card.

(continued)

3. Display the word-of-the-day calendar on a bulletin board or wall and place five of the phrase cards in the pockets (one card per pocket) with the words facing in. Each morning, turn over the card in that day's pocket to reveal the "magic" words. Challenge children to use the word or expression at least three times throughout the day. At the end of the week, you can rearrange the word cards or use new ones.

Friendship Coupons

Inspire acts of kindness with vocabulary-building coupons.

1. Photocopy a supply of the friendship coupons (page 22). Cut apart coupons and place in a basket labeled "Friendship Coupons."

2. When children want to express thanks or appreciation for one another, invite them to fill out a coupon and present it to their friend. Encourage children to use their coupons both in school and out, all year long!

Household Words

Build home-based vocabulary as children learn to sort and classify words.

1. Make a copy of the house template (page 23; enlarge first, if desired) for each child. To build the house, help children cut on the dashed lines to make flaps; the flaps will create windows and a door that can be open and closed. Be sure not to cut on the solid lines.

2. Next, instruct children to glue the house template to a sheet of plain paper, making sure not to glue down any of the flaps. Have children write their name on the line. If they like, children can also color the outside of the house.

3. Now it's time to add the "household words." Explain to children that just as people can belong to a family, words can belong to a family. For instance, *lion*, *tiger*, *bear*, and *zebra* are all names of animals. For this

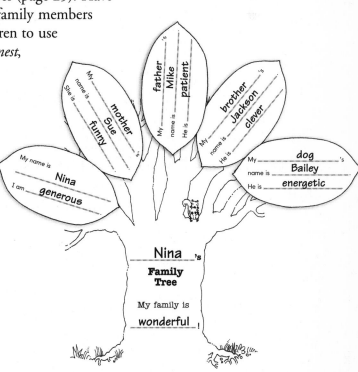

activity, children will be writing a group of six words that belong together, and they will all be about houses.

4. Help children suggest categories of words related to houses, such as rooms in a home (*bedroom, bathroom, kitchen, family room*); types of homes (*house, apartment, igloo, tepee, hut*); furniture (*chair, table, couch, desk*); and household chores (*laundry, sweeping, dusting, mopping*).

5. Have children choose a category, open the window and door flaps, and write or dictate a word from that category in the space underneath each flap. When children are finished, let them explore each other's homes by opening the flaps. Encourage children to guess the category of words that each house holds!

My Family Tree

Plant the seeds for family vocabulary with this activity.

1. Give each child a copy of the family tree template (page 24). Have children write their name on the trunk of their tree.

2. Next, discuss the concept of family with children. A family can be the people who live with you, but it can also include people who live far away. Mostly, a family is a group of people who love and care about one another.

3. Invite children to think about the people who make up their family. Make a list of "family" words—for example, *mother, father, grandmother, uncle, sister, big brother,* and *dog.*

4. Give each child a copy of the family tree leaves (page 25). Have children fill in the blanks to tell about their family members and then cut out the leaves. Encourage children to use character-trait words such as *loving, kind, honest, funny,* and *athletic* to complete line 3. Note that some children may need more than one copy of the leaf patterns. Remind children to create a leaf for themselves.

5. Have children glue their leaves on the tree. Then have them write a word on the trunk to describe their family as a whole (*active, fun-loving, noisy*). Children can also decorate the tree with crayons if desired.

6. Display children's trees on a bulletin board or wall to create a "family orchard." Encourage children to explore one another's families and the words that describe them.

Friendship Coupon

To _____   From _____

You're my friend, and I'm yours, too,
and here is what I like about you:

_____

So here is something I will do
to show how much I care for you:

_____

Friendship Coupon

To _____   From _____

You're my friend, and I'm yours, too,
and here is what I like about you:

_____

So here is something I will do
to show how much I care for you:

_____

   Vocabulary Activities Just for Young Learners © 2009 Pamela Chanko, Scholastic Teaching Resources

_____'s Household Words

HOME
Sweet
HOME

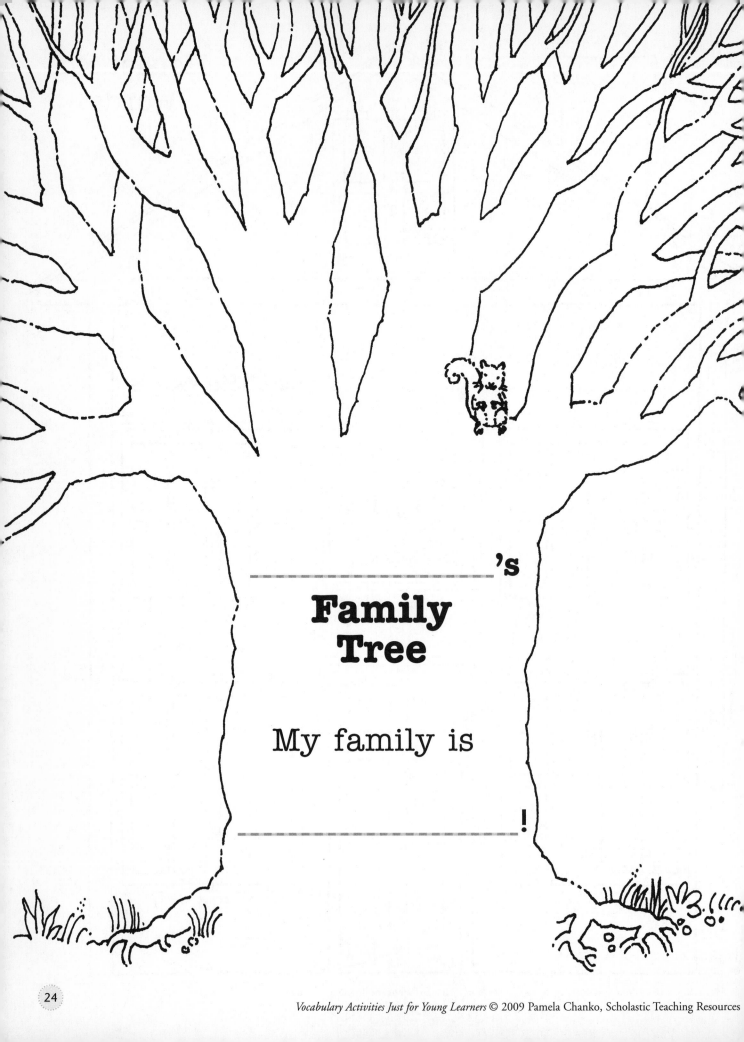

_____'s

Family Tree

My family is

_____!

Family Tree
Leaves

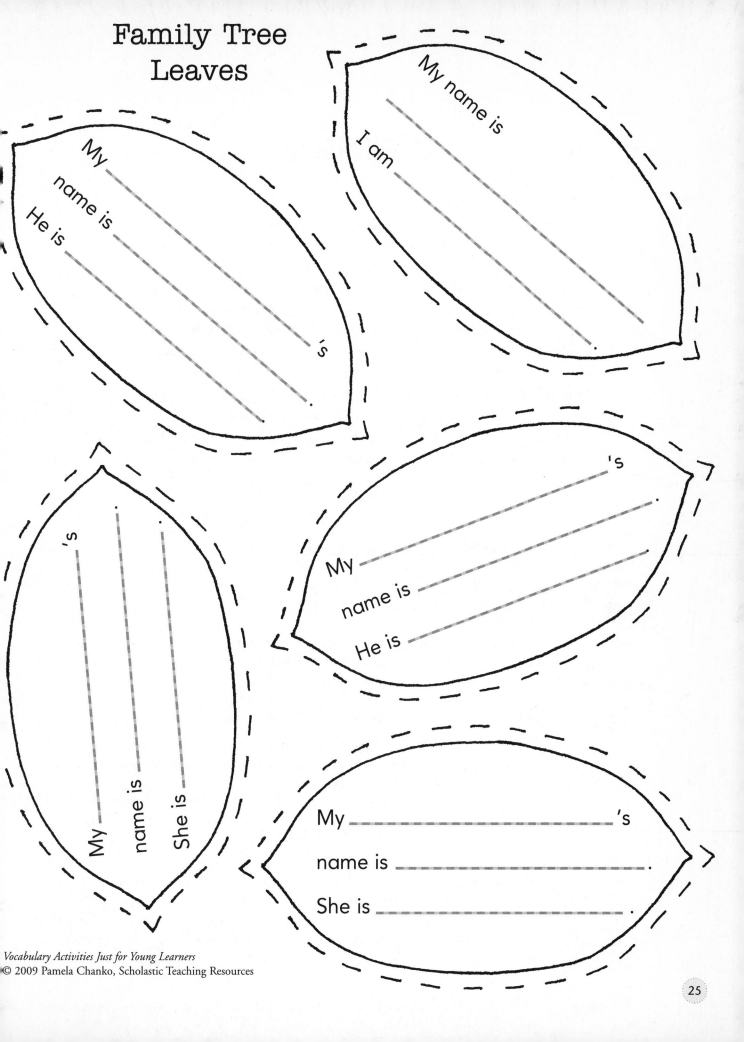

My name is _____
I am _____.

My
name is _____
He is _____'s.

My _____'s
name is _____.
He is _____.

My _____'s
name is _____.
She is _____.

My _____'s
name is _____.
She is _____.

Feelings

From happy to sad to angry to glad, human emotions run the gamut. There are many words to describe feelings, and each one has a slightly different shade of meaning. It's important to teach children emotional vocabulary, not only for the word power, but also because it provides children with a solid tool for self-expression. Children who are able to express their feelings articulately benefit in all sorts of areas and situations, at school and in the home. Pay close attention to children's day-to-day experiences, providing them with words to express their emotions as they occur. For instance, if a child is struggling with a difficult math problem and says he is "mad," you might mention that he seems *frustrated*. A child who says she is "happy" after scoring a home run in the softball game might be described as *exhilarated*. When children learn words about their own feelings, they have a unique opportunity to internalize the meaning of the word—because the definition lies within themselves.

Feelings and Faces Book

In this collaborative book, children practice "making faces" to express a variety of emotions.

1. Begin a discussion about facial expressions. Ask: "How does your face look when you are happy? Sad? Angry? What other feelings do you have faces for?" Brainstorm words for feelings and list on chart paper. In addition to familiar words such as *happy* and *sad*, suggest vocabulary words such as *calm, frustrated, disappointed, excited,* and *amazed*.

2. Give each child a copy of the Feelings and Faces Book template (page 30) and read the poem aloud. Invite children to choose a word from the list to fill in the blank, or use a word of their own. Provide crayons, yarn, and collage materials and have children create a self-portrait on the blank face to show the emotion. If possible, give children hand mirrors to guide their illustrations. They can make faces in the mirror and then draw what they see!

3. When children are finished, gather their pages and cut sheets of construction paper for the covers. Give the book a title, such as "Our Many Faces," and bind the pages with staples or yarn. Invite children to read the book, identify each emotion, and imitate each face they see.

What's That You Say?

Use emotional vocabulary to liven up speech tags.

1. Dialogue is a tricky part of writing, whether children are writing an independent story or doing a shared writing activity with the group. Often, dialogue can become repetitive, with the words *he said* and *she said* appearing over and over. Gather picture books or read-aloud stories that contain lots of dialogue and work with children to hunt for speech tags that express emotion, such as *he grumbled, she exclaimed,* and *they shouted.* Write each verb on an index card.

2. Work together to come up with more verbs. You can spark ideas by giving children scenarios, for instance: "If you were telling someone a secret, how would you describe the voice you would use?" (*whisper*) "What if you were trying to tell somebody something who was far away?" (*yell*) Suggest additional words, such as *whooped, questioned, shrieked,* and *murmured,* and write these on cards as well.

3. Place the speech-tag verbs on a wall or bulletin board and encourage children to use them in their independent and collaborative writing.

If You're Happy and You Know It

Build vocabulary by writing new lyrics to a familiar song.

1. Teach children the following song:

    If you're happy and you know it, clap your hands (clap, clap).
    If you're happy and you know it, clap your hands (clap, clap).
    If you're happy and you know it, and you really want to show it
    If you're happy and you know it, clap your hands (clap, clap).

2. After singing the song a few times, say, "People sometimes clap their hands when they're happy. What action might you do if you were sad?" Discuss responses such as "make a frown" and "wipe your eyes." Then sing a new verse of the song, replacing the word *happy* with *sad* and the phrase *clap your hands* with an action children suggested. Encourage children to perform the action after each line.

3. Continue inventing new verses, using more and more sophisticated vocabulary and actions. Examples follow.

    ✳ If you're impatient and you know it, drum your fingers...
    ✳ If you're embarrassed and you know it, hide your eyes...
    ✳ If you're furious and you know it, stamp your feet...

Teaching Tip

▲ ▲ ▲ ▲ ▲ ▲

You can also give children dialogue practice by collecting comic strips. Invite children to rephrase the words in the speech bubbles as dialogue, adding an appropriate speech tag depending on the character's facial expression.

Follow the Feelings! Game

This fun game invites children to match feelings to situations.

1. To set up the game, make one copy of the game board (page 31), and then copy and cut out the game cards (page 32). For durability, you may want to glue the board and cards to card stock or laminate. To complete the spinner on the game board, place a paper clip in the center and then push a paper fastener through the center hole. (Make sure not to fasten too tightly; the paper clip should spin easily.) Gather game markers, such as different colored buttons.

2. Before children play, you may want to review the vocabulary words on the game board and discuss their meaning. Encourage children to give examples of situations in which they might experience each emotion. Then teach groups of two or three children how to play the game, as follows.

Follow the Feelings! Game Directions

1. Each player puts a marker on a "Start" space. Shuffle the game cards and deal each player four cards. The remaining cards are placed facedown in the center of the board.

2. The first player spins the spinner and moves that many spaces along the game board, in the direction of the arrows. If the player lands on a "Start" space, he or she skips a turn.

3. If the player lands on a "Face" space, the player reads the emotion and then looks at his or her cards. If the player has a situation card that matches the emotion, the player reads it aloud and then discards it by placing it facedown at the bottom of the deck. If not, the player must draw another card from the deck.

4. If the new card matches, the player discards it by placing it at the bottom of the deck. If not, the player must keep the card.

5. Then it is the next player's turn. Players continue taking turns until one player has no cards left.

Important Note: In order for a player to discard, all players must agree that the situation matches the emotion. Remember that different players may have different feelings. For instance, one player might feel *nervous* if he or she got the lead in the school play, while another might be *joyful, amazed,* or *excited.* As long as the player can explain the emotion to everyone's satisfaction, he or she may discard.

Face in a Frame Relay

Children act out a variety of emotions in this fast-paced game.

1. In advance, obtain an old, empty picture frame, large enough to surround children's faces. (Make sure there are no sharp edges and make sure to remove any glass.) Then write a variety of words for feelings on small slips of paper. You can include basic feelings, such as *happy, sad,* and *surprised,* as well as more nuanced feelings, such as *annoyed, relieved,* and *jumpy.* Review each word with children, and then place all the slips in a paper bag.

2. Lean the frame against a wall of the classroom and stand next to it, holding the paper bag. Line children up at a short distance. When you say "Go," the first child runs to you, selects a slip of paper, and then holds up the frame and makes a face to illustrate the feeling.

3. Anyone in the group can guess the word the child is acting out. As soon as the word is guessed correctly, it's the next child's turn.

4. Play until each word has been guessed, or until each child has had a turn. Then do the relay again, challenging children to beat their time!

Feel Like a Snack?

Here's a fun, quick way to work feelings vocabulary into snack time.

1. Give each child a rice cake or half of an English muffin, and set out cream cheese or another spread along with raisins, apple slices, banana rounds, or any other foods that can be used to create features. Be sure to check for food allergies first.

2. Have children choose a feeling, spread the topping on their rice cake or muffin, and then use the other ingredients to create features—for example, using raisins for eyes, apple slices for smiles or frowns, or a banana round for a nose.

3. Before children eat, invite them to look at one another's creations. Let the group guess which feeling each snack represents, and then let children reveal the feeling they chose.

Name _____

I have many faces—

Here's one for our book.

When I'm feeling

_____ ,

This is how I look!

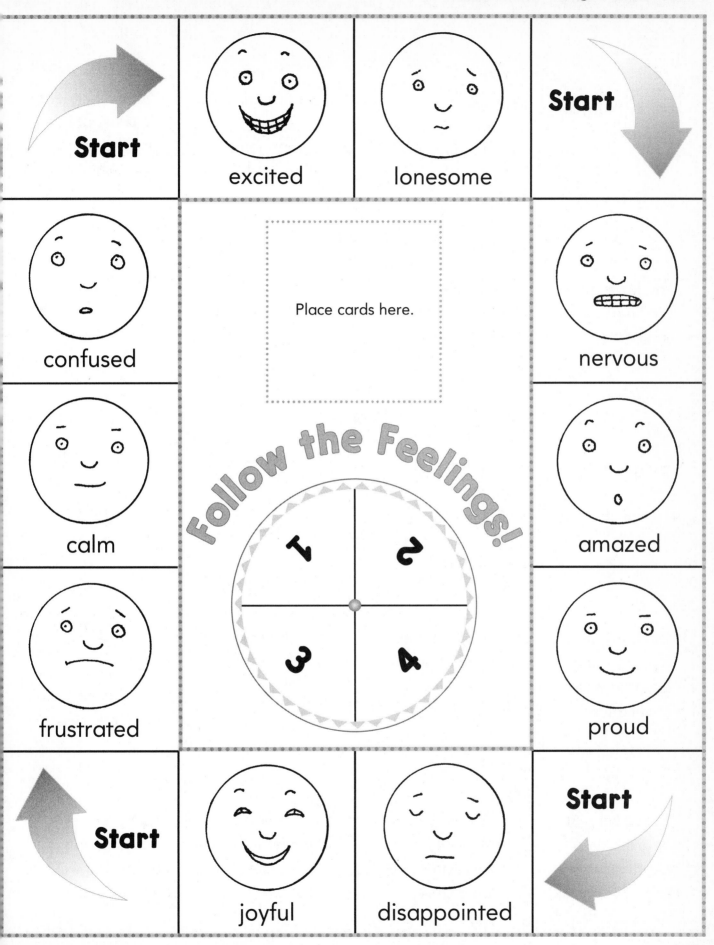

Follow the Feelings! Game Cards

Your birthday is tomorrow.	You just got the lead in the school play.	Your friends are at a party, but you are home with a cold.	Your best friend is away at camp for the whole summer.
You have a big spelling test tomorrow.	You have to give a report in front of your class.	You see a camel in your backyard.	You just won a prize in the school raffle.
You got a good grade on a math test.	You made the winning goal in the soccer game.	You did not get the gift you wanted for your birthday.	You can't go on your picnic because it is raining.
You just found out you will get an extra week of vacation.	Your teacher just told you there will be no homework for a month.	You are learning to ride a bike, and you keep falling off.	You want to get someone's attention, but the person won't listen to you.
You are lying in the grass on a beautiful summer day.	You are lying in bed while someone reads you a story.	You are watching a movie and you can't understand the story.	Your friend is teaching you a game, but the rules are unclear.

Vocabulary Activities Just for Young Learners © 2009 Pamela Chanko, Scholastic Teaching Resources

The Five Senses

As children move up through the grades, they will be asked to write in more and more sophisticated ways. And as every teacher knows, a key to good writing is the use of sensory imagery—that is, the use of words that relate to sight, smell, taste, touch, and sound. There's no better way to prepare children for this challenge than by giving them the descriptive vocabulary they'll need. Children learn naturally through their experiences of the world that surrounds them, and it's never too early to help them learn ways to articulate those experiences. If a child describes his favorite stuffed animal as "soft," you can introduce the words *fluffy* and *fuzzy*. If a child says a noise is "loud," you might introduce words such as *booming* or *thundering*. These sorts of teachable moments can occur all day long, and with repetition even the most sophisticated word can become part of children's vocabulary. As you introduce new words, be sure to apply them to a variety of situations. For instance, if you mention that a blanket feels *downy*, you might also use the word to describe the feathers on a baby chick, or even the soft fuzz on the outside of a peach. The more contexts in which children hear and use a word, the more likely they are to internalize it.

Gimme Five!

Try this board game to strengthen children's sense-related vocabulary.

1. Copy the game board (page 37) and the game cards (pages 38–39). To make the game cards, cut out along the dashed lines only. Then fold each card in half and paste together so that the sense icon (eye, ear, nose, mouth, hand) is on one side and the adjective is on the other. Laminate the board and cards if desired.

2. Prepare children for playing the game by having a quick discussion about the five senses. Talk about which body part they use for each sense, and then discuss the different ways they can describe tastes, textures, sights, smells, and sounds. Review the vocabulary words on the game cards and ask children to give examples. For instance, the sun looks *bright*; a pretzel tastes *salty*; a dirty sock smells *stinky*; a snowball feels *cold*; and a mouse sounds *squeaky*.

3. Gather a game marker for each player (such as different colored buttons or math cubes) and a penny for each group of two to four players. Explain how to play the game. (See Game Directions, page 34.)

(continued)

Teaching Tip

For more taste-related vocabulary activities, see the Food theme unit (page 40).

Gimme Five! Game Directions

1 Separate the cards into five piles, one for each sense. Mix up the cards in each pile, and place them with the body part facing up. Put the card piles within reach of all players. Each player puts a marker on the "Start" space.

2 The first player tosses the penny. If it lands heads up, the player moves ahead two spaces. If it lands tails up, the player moves ahead one space.

3 The player reads the directions on the space and picks the top card off the appropriate pile to complete the sentence. For example, if the space says "Name something that tastes..." the player picks the top card off the "mouth" pile and then turns it over to read the word.

4 The player must then name something that could be described by that word. For instance, if the player is asked to name something that tastes *tangy*, he or she might say "orange juice."

5 If all players agree with the choice of item, the player stays on the space. If not, or if the player cannot think of an item, the player moves back one space. (Players cannot use previously named items.) The player then places the card back at the bottom of the pile it was chosen from.

6 Then it is the next player's turn. Players continue taking turns until one player reaches the "Finish" space.

Fold-'em-Up Guessing Game

Build descriptive vocabulary with a sensory guessing game.

1. In advance, cut plain drawing paper into $8\frac{1}{2}$- x $8\frac{1}{2}$-inch squares, one for each child. Give each child a square, and provide pencils and crayons or markers.

2. Guide children in following steps 1 through 5.

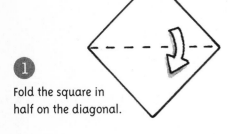

1 Fold the square in half on the diagonal.

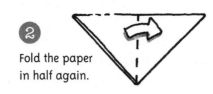

2 Fold the paper in half again.

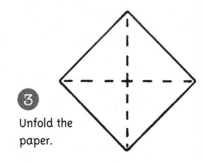

3 Unfold the paper.

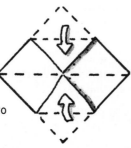

4 Fold the top and bottom corners into the center point.

 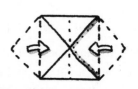

5 Fold in both side corners.

3. Have children choose something that they can describe well using sensory words. It can be anything from an ice-cream cone to a puppy. Then have children choose four sensory words to describe the item and write one word on each triangle. For instance, for *pizza*, a child might write "round" (sight), "cheesy" (taste), "spicy" (smell), and "gooey" (touch).

4. When children have written their words, have them unfold the corners of their paper. In the center of the paper, children can draw a picture of their item and label it (see sample, right). Finally, have children fold the corners back in, so the words are displayed but the picture is hidden.

5. Have children trade papers with one another, read the four descriptive words, and guess the item. Children can then unfold the corners to check their guess.

Sing About Sounds!

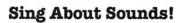

Introduce the concept of onomatopoeia with this activity.

1. To begin, introduce the word *onomatopoeia*, saying each syllable slowly and having children repeat after you. Then explain that the term onomatopoeia refers to words that imitate sounds. Ask, "What sound does a dog make?" (*woof, arf*) "What about a cat?" (*meow*)

2. Together, brainstorm a list of additional onomatopoetic words and list them on chart paper. Include words such as *buzz, crackle, pop, crunch, swish, beep, hum,* and *splash*. Next to each word, write the name of something that makes the sound (for instance: *crunch–carrot; crackle–fire; beep-car*).

3. Now it's time to put your words to music! Sing this song to the tune of "Old McDonald Had a Farm." For every verse, insert a new child's name and a new object and sound, such as *rubber band/boing, keyboard/click, breeze/whoosh,* and *faucet/drip*. Use objects and sounds from your list, and work together to come up with more as needed. As an extension, invite children to write or dictate a short story including as many sound words as they can.

> Young (**child's name**) wrote a story, E-I-E-I-O.
> And in this story there was a **horn**, E-I-E-I-O.
> With a **toot-toot** here, and a **toot-toot** there,
> Here a **toot**, there a **toot**, everywhere a **toot-toot**,
> Young (**child's name**) wrote a story, E-I-E-I-O.

Making Sense of Similes

Introduce figurative language that appeals to the senses.

1. Introduce the word *simile*. Explain that a simile is an expression that compares one thing to something else. Ask, "Have you ever heard the expression 'as big as a house'? What do you think it means?" (*very large*) Point out that this simile describes how something looks. Then introduce similes that appeal to the senses of touch, taste, and sound, for instance: *as soft as a kitten*; *as sweet as a peach*; *as quiet as a mouse*.

2. Write the following fill-in on several sentence strips: *as ____ as a/an ____*. With the class, come up with adjectives for the first blank, such as *smooth, bumpy, sour, spicy, noisy, quiet, tiny*, and *flat*. List them on chart paper.

3. Divide the class into small groups and give each group a sentence strip. Invite each group to choose a word from the list and write it in the first blank. Then have children work together to come up with an appropriate word for the second blank. For instance, if children choose the word *sour*, they might complete the simile with *lemon*; if they choose the word *tiny*, they might complete the simile with *flea*. Invite children to illustrate their similes and then share them with the group.

Roll-a-Sense

This game builds vocabulary and inspires creative thinking.

1. Make game cubes by covering two empty cube-shaped tissue boxes with construction paper. On one cube, write the following words, one per side: *sight, smell, sound, touch*, and *taste*. On the sixth side, write *roll again*. On the second cube, write the names of places. Choose locales that will inspire lots of sensory words, such as *playground, jungle, mall, forest, zoo*, and *beach*.

2. Seat children in a circle and model how to play the game by tossing both cubes. The goal is to name an item that you can taste, hear, touch, smell, or see in a particular place, and then describe it. So, if you rolled *taste* and *beach*, you might name *water* and describe the taste as *salty*. If you rolled *forest* and *sound*, you might name *birds* and describe the sound as *chirping*. Tell children that if the senses cube lands on "roll again," they should roll only that cube again until it lands on a sense.

3. Let children take turns rolling the cubes and describing senses in various places. Remind children that there is no "winner" in this game—the object is simply to have fun with words. So, if a child is stumped on his or her turn, the whole group can discuss ideas. Continue the game until each child has had a chance to roll the cubes.

Name something that **feels**…

Name something that **tastes**…

Name something that **looks**…

Name something that **smells**…

START

Name something that **sounds**…

Name something that **looks**…

Name something that **tastes**…

Name something that **feels**…

Name something that **smells**…

Name something that **sounds**…

Name something that **tastes**…

Gimme Five!
Game Board

FINISH

Name something that **sounds**…

Name something that **looks**…

Name something that **tastes**…

Name something that **feels**…

Name something that **smells**…

Name something that **tastes**…

Name something that **sounds**…

Name something that **feels**…

Name something that **looks**…

abulary Activities Just for Young Learners
2009 Pamela Chanko, Scholastic Teaching Resources

shiny	bright
sweet	salty
fresh	smoky
rough	smooth
noisy	hushed

dark

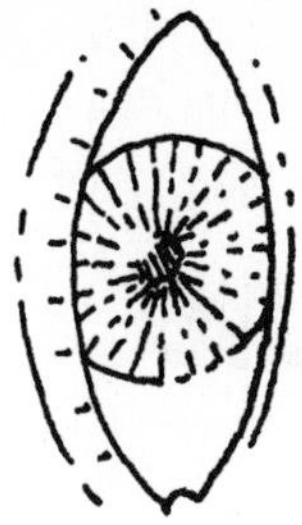

colorful

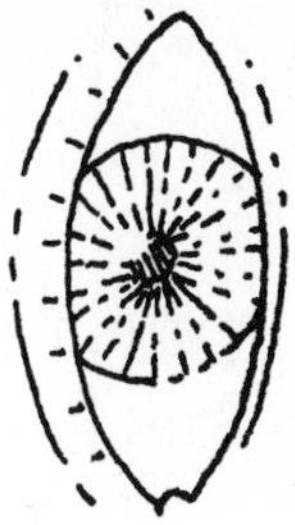

spicy

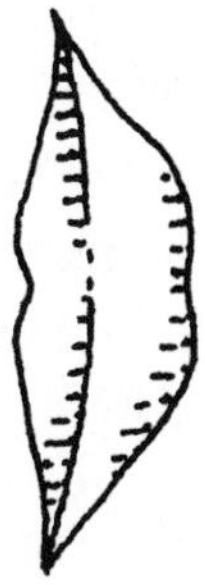

tangy

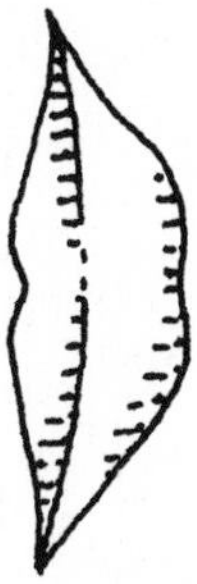

flowery

stinky

hot

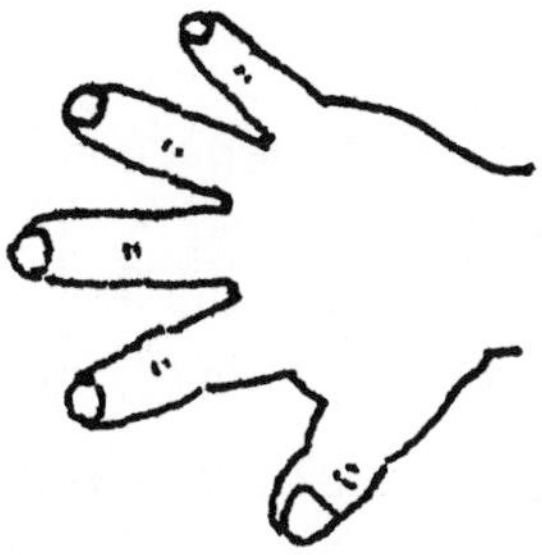

cold

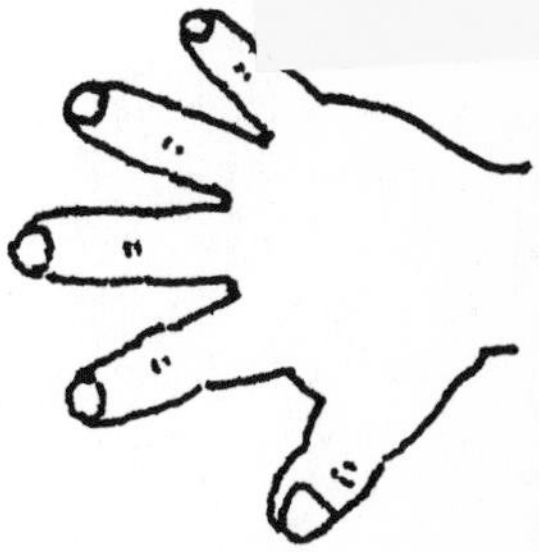

squeaky

rumbling

Food

Food is a wonderfully rich theme for vocabulary building, simply because almost everyone loves to talk about it! Whether your favorite treats are crunchy, creamy, sweet, or savory, the incredible variety of foods available makes it a consistently interesting topic of conversation. Take advantage of vocabulary-building opportunities at the snack or lunch table, inviting children to describe what they are eating and how it tastes. Encourage children to build bridges between vocabulary words by asking questions: "That looks like a salty snack. What are some other snacks that are salty?" Invite children to use descriptive language by saying, "I'm not sure how I would describe this sandwich. What would you say about it?" Take opportunities to introduce sophisticated vocabulary; for instance, when children say a food is "good," you can suggest words such as *delicious, scrumptious, tasty, luscious,* or *flavorful.*

What's My Snack?

With this activity, children build food-related vocabulary through questions and answers.

1. Begin by writing names of foods on separate index cards, such as *banana, chocolate chip cookie,* and *peanut butter and jelly sandwich.* You can also draw a simple picture of the food on each card (or use a sticker or picture cut from a magazine or old workbook).

2. Attach one card to each child's back (without letting children see the card). Then have children move about the classroom, asking questions of their classmates to try to figure out their food. The catch is, children can only ask questions with yes or no answers. For instance, a child can ask "Am I yellow?" but not "What color am I?"

3. Encourage children to ask questions of several classmates before they make their guesses. Once children have guessed their own food, they can remain in the game to answer other children's questions.

Food Flyer Place Mats

Here's a wonderful way to encourage vocabulary building at meal times.

1. Collect old magazines and supermarket flyers. Leaf through a flyer and show children the variety of descriptive words used in food product advertisements, such as *lip-smacking, cheesy, fruity,* and *mouthwatering.*

2. Give each child a large sheet of construction paper, scissors, and glue. Have children look through the magazines and flyers for foods described with unusual or evocative words (children may need help reading some words). Children can then cut out the food pictures along with the words, and glue them on their paper.

3. When dry, laminate children's place mats, or cover with clear contact paper. Have children use the place mats at snack or lunchtime. They can look at their place mat for the perfect word to describe what they're eating! You can rotate the place mats at each meal so that children get to see a variety of vocabulary words.

We're Going on a Picnic

The more students hear a word, the better they will remember it, and in this game, they repeat important words again and again.

1. Seat children in a circle and choose a food that can be described with many different words (such as oranges). Say, "We're going on a picnic, and I'm bringing oranges."

2. Invite the child to your left to add a descriptive word and repeat the sentence, for instance: "We're going on a picnic, and I'm bringing juicy oranges." The next child in the circle repeats the previous words and adds a new word, for instance: "We're going on a picnic, and I'm bringing juicy, sweet oranges."

3. Continue around the circle, with each child repeating the words that came before and adding a new one. You may end up with a sentence like: "We're going on a picnic, and I'm bringing juicy, sweet, tangy, orange, bumpy, seeded, tart, slurpy oranges!" When the word chain is broken (either because the sentence is too long to remember or children are stumped for additional words), the next child can start a new round by naming a different food.

Design-a-Box

Invite children to invent and describe their own breakfast cereal.

1. Gather several clean, empty cereal boxes (you may want to send a note home to family members asking for donations). Invite children to look at the

(continued)

different boxes, and ask questions such as: "What words do you see that describe the cereal? What words have you seen or heard in advertisements for breakfast cereal?" Discuss suggestions such as "sweet, crunchy flakes" and "plump, juicy raisins."

2. Divide the class into small groups, providing each with a cereal box, pencils, and crayons or markers. Have groups decide on a cereal to create, and invent a brand name. Then have children sketch a design on scrap paper, using illustrations and descriptive words to let shoppers know all about their cereal. Encourage children to use evocative words, expressions, and similes, such as "So crunchy it's like a thunderstorm for your mouth!"

3. When children are ready to create their final product, help them cover their box with white construction paper. Then have children work together to put the design on the box. When children are finished, let them present their new cereal to the class!

Tasty Acrostics

Describe favorite treats with acrostic poetry.

1. Have children name their favorite foods as you list them on chart paper.

2. Choose one food and spell it out down the left side of a fresh sheet of chart paper. Then challenge children to think of a word or phrase related to the food that begins with each letter. (See sample, right.)

3. When your poem is complete, read it aloud together. Once children are familiar with the process, they can work individually or in small groups to write poems about the other foods on your list.

Special treat
Piping hot
Add some sauce
Great with meatballs
Hearty meal
Elongated noodles
Twisty
Twirly
Irresistible

Mystery Menu

Create a restaurant menu in which customers have to guess the daily specials!

1. Give each child a copy of the Mystery Menu template (page 44). Provide children with sheets of plain drawing paper, scissors, pencils, crayons, and glue. To prepare the menu, have children cut along the

dashed lines to make a lift-up flap at the bottom of the page. Then have children glue the page to a sheet of drawing paper, without gluing down the flap.

2. Encourage children to think of a food they would like to serve at their restaurant. Have them lift up the flap and draw and label their food in the space underneath. Then, have them write descriptive clues about the food by filling in the blanks at the top of the page. For instance, a child who drew a piece of watermelon might describe the colors as *pink, black*, and *green*; the texture as *juicy*; the taste as *sweet*; and say that it's a good food to eat when *you're hot and sweaty on a summer afternoon*. To finish the page, have children write their name on the top line.

3. When children have completed their pages, staple them together along the left side and create a cover to make a class book of menus. Invite children to read about the "specials," guess the food, and then lift the flap to check their guesses.

Name That Food!

In this game, children describe foods without using "forbidden" words.

1. Make a copy of the game cards (page 45) for each group of four to six children. Cut apart the cards and place them in a basket or bag. Guide children in following steps 2 through 4 to play.

2. Each group splits up into two even teams. The first player on the first team picks a card from the bag and silently shows it to the other team. The player must then describe the secret food for his or her own team *without* using any form of the food name, or the "forbidden" words listed beneath "Without saying." This means that players must find inventive, specific ways to describe the food on their card.

3. The other players on the team try to guess the secret food from the clue-giver's description. If they can guess the food correctly, their team earns a point. It's the opposing team's job to listen carefully. If the clue-giver uses a "forbidden" word, they shout "Forbidden Word!" and their team earns the point.

4. Once a point is earned from the card (or if neither team can earn a point), it is discarded. Then the first player from the second team picks a card for the next round. Teams continue to take turns and rotate clue-givers until all the cards have been used. The team with the most points wins the game.

Teaching Tip

▲▲▲▲▲▲

Expand the game by giving children index cards and having each team create additional game cards for the other team to use.

_____ 's Diner

Today's special is . . .

Color: _____

Texture: _____

Taste: _____

Good to eat when _____

_____

Describe a . . .

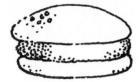

(**hamburger**)

Without saying...

bun

meat

ketchup

Describe a . . .

(**lollipop**)

Without saying...

round

sweet

lick

Describe a . . .

(**birthday cake**)

Without saying...

candles

icing

wish

Describe a . . .

(**plate of spaghetti**)

Without saying...

noodles

long

tomato sauce

Describe an . . .

(**apple**)

Without saying...

crunchy

red

seeds

Describe an . . .

(**ice cream cone**)

Without saying...

cold

scoop

melt

Describe a . . .

(**donut**)

Without saying...

hole

round

dunk

Describe a . . .

(**glass of milk**)

Without saying...

cold

white

cow

Describe a . . .

(**pizza**)

Without saying...

pie

cheese

crust

Jobs

As every teacher knows, the idea of becoming a "grown-up" is fascinating to children, and this includes "grown-up" jobs. The world of work is a high-interest topic that children enjoy exploring through books and pretend play, and it also provides a great opportunity for vocabulary building. Because occupations are generally for adults, the vocabulary associated with those occupations is naturally mature. And because children watch adults doing their jobs every day, they have concrete examples that help them internalize high-level words such as *librarian*, *astronaut*, *carpenter*, and *veterinarian*. You can help children build vocabulary by discussing the jobs they see people do, and the jobs they'd like to do themselves one day.

Hats on the Job Wheel

Invite children to try on hats to become a firefighter, a police officer, or even a chef, and build occupational vocabulary.

1. Give each child a copy of the Hats on the Job Wheel patterns (pages 50–51). Help children cut out both parts of the wheel. (For a more durable wheel, copy onto card stock.)

2. To prepare the top wheel, provide children with markers and crayons and invite them to color the figure to look like themselves. Children can draw a face, hair, and clothing. Help children cut on the dashed lines to create a flap.

3. Invite children to color in the hats on the bottom wheel if they wish. When they are finished, have children place the top wheel over the bottom wheel. Help them insert a brass fastener through the center.

4. Now let children turn the top wheel to "try on" different hats. Invite them to read the sentence and name the occupation. Then have children lift the flap to check their guess.

Help Wanted!

Boost writing and vocabulary skills by turning a bulletin board into the classified section of a newspaper.

1. Give each child a copy of the Help Wanted! template (page 52). Before children begin, discuss the purpose of a classified ad. Explain that when someone needs a worker, he or she can put an ad in the newspaper. Then someone who wants to do the job can answer the ad. Tell children that they will be creating their own "help wanted" ads.

2. First, have children cut the sheet along the dashed line. Encourage them to fill out the bottom portion by writing a job of their choice on the line. Then have children color the figure to look like a person who does that job. For instance, if children wrote *doctor*, they might draw a white coat and a stethoscope around the doctor's neck. If children wrote *construction worker*, they might dress the figure in a hard hat and a tool belt.

3. Next, invite children to fill in the blanks on the top portion of the page to tell details about the job (without naming it).

4. When children are finished, collect the top portion of their sheets and post them on an eye-level bulletin board. Then place the "job applications" (the bottoms of the sheets) in a paper bag. Let each child choose one, and then have children study the ads on the board. When children find a want ad that matches, they can respond to the ad by attaching their "application" beneath it.

Help Wanted!

Looking for someone who can __cook good food__

At your job, you will use __spoons, bowls, and an oven__

You will wear __a tall white hat__

The place you will work is __a kitchen__

Apply Today!

I can do it! I am a __chef__!

Meet the Staff

Add a vocabulary-building twist to your classroom job rotation.

1. You can make classroom jobs more "grown-up" by giving children official job titles. If you already have a job system in place, review the different jobs with children and discuss what each one entails. If your students do not already do class jobs, create a job for each child. Jobs can include being the line leader, watering plants, and setting up snack.

2. Next, tell children that grown-ups usually have job titles. A job title is a name for a job, just like a book title is a name for a book. Often, job titles use special vocabulary, and many of them contain very big words! Tell children you will introduce some "big words" that they can use for

(continued)

their own job titles. Use the list at right to introduce children to their new titles, explaining each vocabulary word in detail. For instance, you can say: "A caterer is someone who makes and sets up the food for parties. What job do we have in our class that has to do with setting up food?" (*snack helper*) "Could we call the person who helps set up the food for snack a caterer?" (*yes*) If you have a class job that is not listed below, you can make up your own job title.

3. Once you've given each classroom job a title, you can create business cards. Simply write the job title on an index card, and the name of the child who does the job above the title. Post the business cards on a job board. You might want to laminate the cards to create a write-on/wipe-off surface. This way you can rotate jobs regularly and reuse the cards.

Classroom Job Titles

✳ **Administrative Assistant:** Passes out and collects papers.

✳ **Assembly-Line Manager:** Leads the line when the class lines up.

✳ **Caterer:** Helps set up snack.

✳ **Census Taker:** Helps take attendance.

✳ **Computer Technician:** Turns on and shuts down classroom computers.

✳ **Electrician:** Turns out lights when the class leaves the classroom.

✳ **Fire Chief:** Leads students in classroom or school fire drills.

✳ **Gardener:** Waters the plants.

✳ **Inventory Specialist:** Helps organize classroom supplies.

✳ **Librarian:** Keeps classroom library organized.

✳ **Meteorologist:** Records the daily weather.

✳ **Veterinarian:** Cares for class pets.

Briefcase Bingo

With this game, make connections between workers and the tools they use.

1. Create a template for a blank bingo board. Depending on children's skill level, you can draw a grid of 9 or 16 squares. Copy a board for each child and provide children with board markers such as dried beans or counters.

2. Brainstorm a list of jobs with children. Write the list on chart paper, including such jobs as *firefighter, doctor, police officer, teacher, mail carrier, chef, painter, construction worker, librarian,* and *dentist.* Have children write a job in each square on their game board. (Be sure children don't write the jobs in the order of your list; all the game boards should be different.)

3. To create the bingo cards, brainstorm a tool that each worker would need in his or her "briefcase" and write each on an index card. For instance, the matching cards for *doctor*, *firefighter*, and *carpenter* might be *stethoscope*, *hose*, and *hammer*, respectively. Place the cards in a paper bag.

4. Pull out the cards one at a time, reading aloud the name of each tool. If children see a worker on their board that would use the tool, they can cover that space. The first child to cover a complete row calls out "Briefcase Bingo!" Then children can clear their boards and play again.

Community Thank-You

Encourage children to give thanks to the people who keep their neighborhood up and running! With this activity, children use job-related vocabulary to write thank-you notes.

1. Discuss with children the people in their school and neighborhood who help them each day. List helpers on the board, such as *crossing guard*, *custodian*, *principal*, *school nurse*, *librarian*, *bus driver*, *mail carrier*, *firefighter*, and *police officer*.

2. Discuss what each of the helpers does. For instance, the crossing guard helps children cross the street safely; the bus driver helps take children to school; the school nurse helps children who are sick.

3. Provide each child with construction paper, crayons, markers, and other art materials. Have children fold the construction paper in half to make a card. Invite each child to choose a helper on the list and draw a picture of that person on the front of the card. On the inside of the card, have children complete these sentences: *Thank you for [what the helper does]. You are a great [name of job]!* Encourage children to use descriptive words that provide details about how each person does his or her job. For instance, children might mention that the veterinarian is *kind* and *gentle* with the animals, or that the mail carrier is always *careful* to deliver the mail to the right address.

4. Have children sign their names and, if possible, deliver their cards. Having their work recognized and appreciated is sure to brighten your neighborhood helpers' day!

Hats on the Job
Wheel

Hats on the Job Wheel

This hat makes me a . . .

?

Vocabulary Activities Just for Young Learners
© 2009 Pamela Chanko, Scholastic Teaching Resources

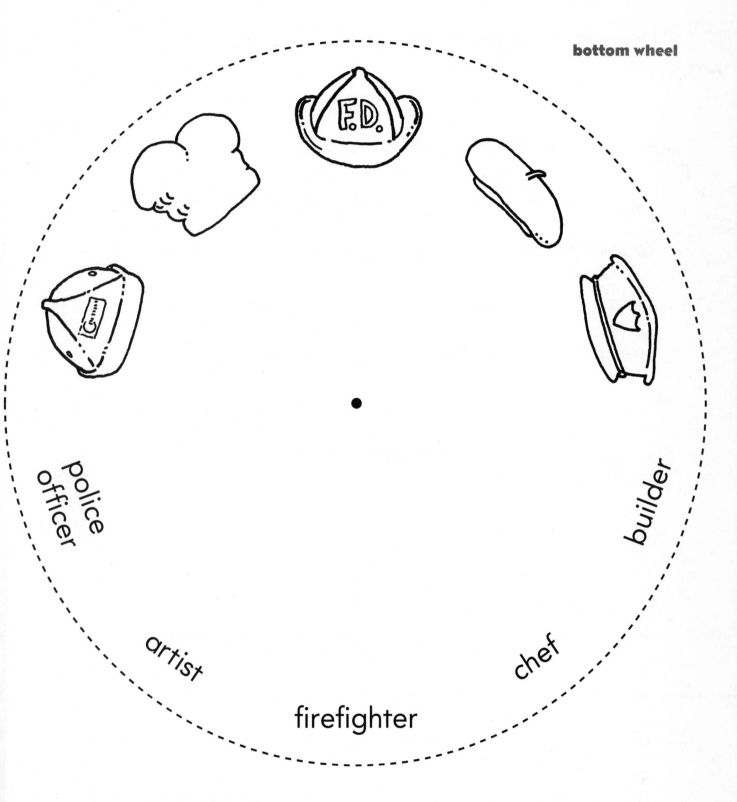

police officer

builder

artist

chef

firefighter

Help Wanted!

Looking for someone who can _____

_____ .

At your job, you will use _____

_____ .

You will wear _____

_____ .

The place you will work is _____

_____ .

Apply Today!

I can do it! I am a _____

Transportation

Cars, trains, trucks, bikes, planes, and boats—children just love talking about things that go! The theme of transportation is a rich source of vocabulary, not only for names of vehicles (*helicopter, ambulance, space shuttle*) but also for precise, active verbs (planes *soar* and *glide*, race cars *speed* and *zoom*, horses *trot* and *gallop*). Children best learn new words when they can relate them to other words, or to words they already know—and transportation words are perfect for this type of association because they can be easily sorted and classified. All vehicles travel on land, water, or air. Therefore, children can easily learn that *airplane, jet,* and *helicopter* are in the same family; as are *car, truck,* and *van*; and *ship, rowboat,* and *canoe*. The subject of travel is also full of excitement. Rather than simply "going" somewhere, children can learn to *wander, explore, journey,* and *cruise*!

Road Race

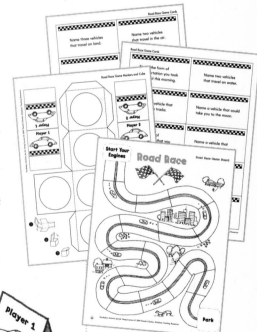

In this game, children race vehicles as they practice transportation vocabulary.

1. To set up the game, copy the game board (page 56; enlarge first to accommodate the game markers) and copy and cut out the car markers and game cards (pages 57–59). If desired, glue the game board and cards to card stock (or laminate them) for durability.

2. To create the game cube, cut it out along the solid line and color two of the circles red, two yellow, and two green. Fold on the dashed lines to make a cube shape. Then fold back the tabs and glue to the inside of the cube to secure. To make the game markers, fold on the center line, fold in the tabs, and glue the tabs one on top of the other (to create "standing" game markers).

3. Teach pairs of children how to play the game. (See Game Directions, page 54.)

(continued)

Road Race Game Directions

1 Shuffle the cards and place them facedown next to the game board. Both players place their markers on the "Start Your Engines" space.

2 The game cube acts as a "traffic light." The first player rolls the cube. If it comes up on red, the player may not move forward, and it is the second player's turn. If it comes up on yellow, the player moves forward one space and takes the top card off the pile. If it comes up on green, the player moves forward two spaces and takes the top card off the pile.

3 The player reads the directions on the card and names an appropriate vehicle or other form of transportation. If both players agree with the answer, the player may stay on that space. If the answer is challenged and judged incorrect, the player must move back one space. The card is then placed back at the bottom of the pile. Then it is the next player's turn.

4 Players continue taking turns until one player reaches the "Park" space.

Sing a Song of Travel

Reinforce transportation vocabulary by creating piggyback words to two favorite tunes.

1. To practice names of vehicles, use "Row, Row, Row Your Boat." Sing the traditional version several times with children. Then introduce new words (see right). You can sing the song over and over, inserting a new vehicle environment, and verb each time—for example: *fly your plane, fly it through the sky; ride your bike, ride it in the park;* and *conduct your train, conduct it on the tracks.*

> Drive, drive, drive your car,
> Drive it down the road.
> Drive it fast or drive it slow.
> That's the way to go!

2. To practice vocabulary for parts of vehicles, use "The Wheels on the Bus." Again, sing the traditional version several times, until children are familiar with the tune and the pattern of the words. Then sing the song about a different vehicle (see below). Continue, inserting new vehicles and parts for each verse—for example: *the siren on the ambulance goes whoo, whoo, whoo; the meter on the taxi goes click, click, click; the hooves on the horse go clop, clop, clop, clop.*

> The hose on the fire truck goes splash, splash, splash,
> Splash, splash, splash, splash, splash, splash.
> The hose on the fire truck goes splash, splash, splash,
> All through the town.

The Best Way to Travel

Build descriptive vocabulary by trying a new twist on a transportation graph.

1. Across the top of a sheet of tagboard, write the names of several vehicles, such as *car, boat, airplane, bicycle, train*, and any other vehicles children might suggest. If you like, you can also add simple pictures.

2. Tell children that they will be "voting" for their favorite form of transportation. But in order to vote, children must think of a word or phrase that describes the vehicle or tells why they like it.

3. Give each child a large sticky note. Have children label their sticky note with their name. Beneath their name, children can write a word or phrase about their vehicle. For instance, a child who chooses "train" might write *noisy and long*.

4. Have children place their notes under the vehicle they chose. Use the graph children create to count how many different vehicles children chose, how many different ways they described the vehicles, and so on.

Street Sign Opposites

Reinforce antonyms by taking your class on the road!

1. If possible, take a walk around your neighborhood to hunt for signs. Otherwise, you can use pictures (a good source is *I Read Signs* by Tana Hoban, HarperCollins, 1987). Make a list of the words that appear on the signs you see and invite children to suggest other signs they may know of.

2. Next, go through your list and challenge children to find pairs of signs that use opposite words or have opposite meanings. Some examples might be *Walk/Don't Walk, East/West, North/South, Exit/Enter,* and *Parking/No Parking.*

3. Invite pairs of children to choose a set of opposites and create the signs from construction paper and crayons. Encourage children to use the same colors and shapes as used on the actual signs.

4. When children are finished, display their signs on a wall or bulletin board in random order, using removable wall adhesive. Challenge children to find the opposites and place each pair side by side.

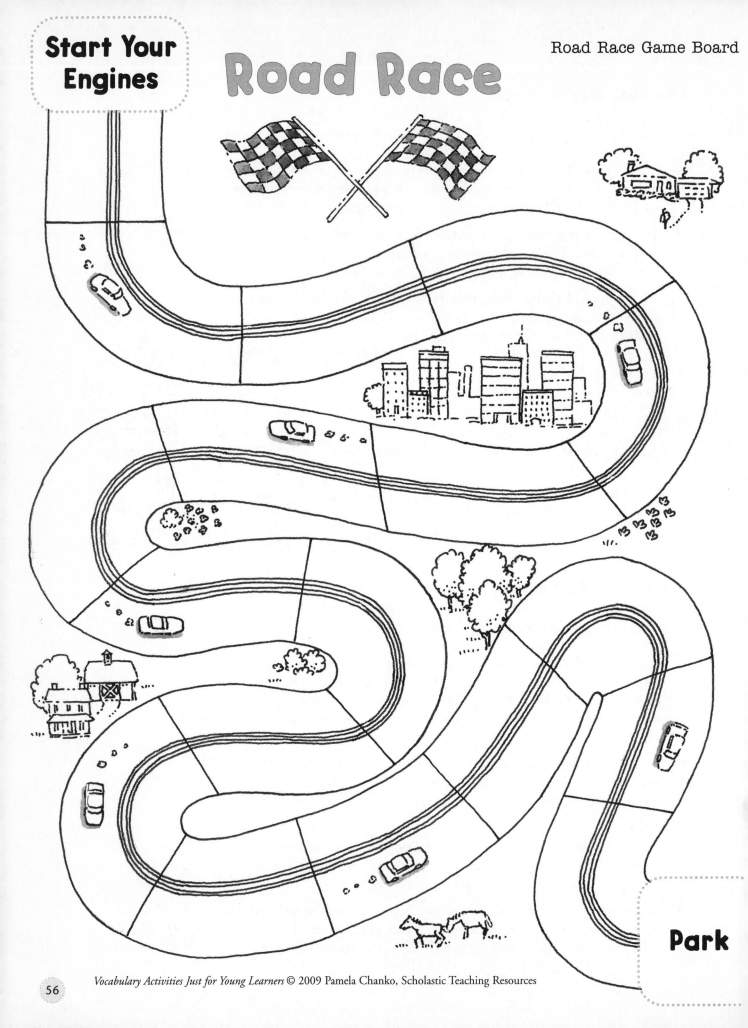

Start Your Engines

Road Race

Park

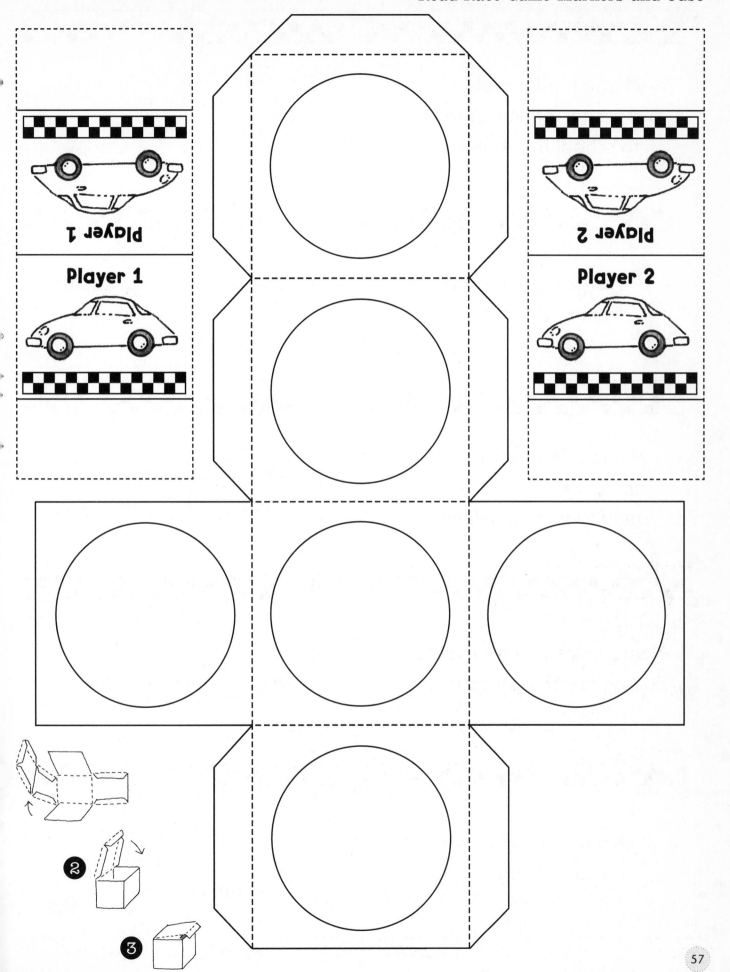

Player 1

Player 2

Name the form of transportation you took to school this morning.

Name two vehicles that travel on water.

Name a vehicle that travels on tracks.

Name a vehicle that could take you to the moon.

Name a form of transportation that you need to wear a helmet for.

Name a vehicle that travels under the ground.

Name an animal that you can ride on for transportation.

Name a vehicle that you might see in a city.

Name a vehicle that has a steering wheel.

Name a vehicle that you might see at a construction site.

Vocabulary Activities Just for Young Learners © 2009 Pamela Chanko, Scholastic Teaching Resources

Name three vehicles that travel on land.

Name two vehicles that travel in the air.

Name a vehicle with two wheels.

Name a vehicle with four wheels.

Name a vehicle that has a siren.

Name a vehicle that has a propeller.

Name a vehicle that you might see in the country.

Name a vehicle that you often see in your neighborhood.

Name a vehicle that you need a ticket to get on.

Name a vehicle that travels on snow.

Animals

Lions and tigers and bears, oh my! The world of animals has always been exciting and magical for children and adults alike, and it's also a subject that's chock-full of wonderful words! After all, there aren't many words that are more fun to say than *platypus*, *hippopotamus*, *rhinoceros*, and *kangaroo*, to name just a few. There are also many interesting names for the places animals live, such as *wetlands*, *rain forest*, *marsh*, and *savannah*. And to top it all off, just think of all the marvelous things animals can do, such as *slither*, *wiggle*, *climb*, *paddle*, *flap*, and *waddle*! When the subject is animals, teachable moments abound, so get children talking (or *squealing*, or *quacking*, or *squawking*) about them!

Snack-Time Stories

With this snack mat, you can turn snack time into a yummy experience filled with vocabulary-building opportunities.

1. Give each child a copy of the Snack-Time Stories Place Mat (page 64). Invite children to color the scene. When children are finished, laminate the place mats for use at the snack table.

2. Purchase a class supply of animal crackers. (Check ingredients for food allergies first.) When it's time for snack, set out the place mats and provide each child with a plastic cup of animal crackers. Encourage children to use their crackers to act out a story as you tell it aloud. Use your story to reinforce names of animals, habitats, and positional words. When the story is over, children can eat up their snacks! Sample stories follow.

   ● A lion and two bears set off on a walk through the woods. The bears followed the path to the cave and went inside. The lion followed the path to the patch of grass and lay down to soak in the sun. Then two hippopotami came out to play in the water. How many animals got wet? How many stayed dry?

   ● Two polar bears followed the path to the icy water. Then a camel walked by. He stopped and talked to the polar bears, and then he walked over to the sunny grass. Soon, an elephant came out to join him. Which animals are in the cold, and which ones are keeping warm?

3. As children become more familiar with following your stories, they can take turns making up their own. You can also use the storytelling mats in a learning center. In this case, substitute toy animals instead of crackers.

Animal Tracks Accordion Book

Invite children to name animals as they create a collaborative rhyming accordion book.

1. Give each child a copy of the Animal Tracks Accordion Book template (page 65). Have each child choose a zoo animal to draw and write about. Suggest exotic animals with interesting names, such as *flamingo*, *ostrich*, *chimpanzee*, *zebra*, and *koala*.

2. Ask children what they think their animal's tracks look like. What shape is the animal's foot? Does it have paws, claws, or webbed feet? Invite children to draw their animal's tracks along the path on the top half of the page. Provide pictures of animal tracks for reference or, if you have toy zoo animals available, children might enjoy dipping the animals in washable paint and then "walking" them across the page.

3. On the bottom half of the page, have children draw a picture of their animal looking out of the frame. Invite them to write their animal's name on both lines. Then have children cut the page in half on the dotted line.

4. When children are finished, collect their work and tape the pages together side by side. Start with an animal track page and follow with the animal's portrait page. Fold the pages back and forth to create an accordion-style book. When complete, children will have their own innovative rhyming animal book. Invite them to read the first page and guess which animal the tracks will lead to. They can then pull to open the next page, look at the animal, and check their guess!

That's a Lot of Lions!

What do you call a bunch of bears? A sleuth! Have fun exploring collective animal nouns with this activity.

1. Introduce collective animal nouns with an example children are likely to be familiar with. For instance, you might say: "To name one bird, you

(continued)

can simply use the word *bird*. But to name a group of birds, you can call them a *flock*. Do you know a word that you can use to name a group of fish?" (*school*)

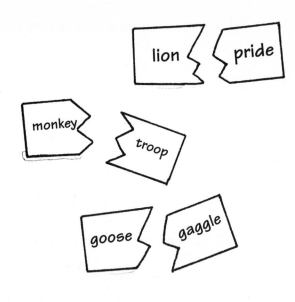

2. Invite children to name their favorite animals. Write each on the left side of an index card. If children know the name for the animal's group, write it on the right side of the card. If not, look it up to find out! (The list below should give you a good start; but keep in mind that many animals have multiple collective noun names. Just one term for each animal group is included here.)

Animal	Group	Animal	Group
cat	clutter	hippopotamus	bloat
bat	colony	hyena	cackle
bear	sleuth	jellyfish	smack
bee	swarm	leopard	leap
bird	flock	lion	pride
dog	pack	monkey	troop
dolphin	pod	parrot	company
elephant	parade	porcupine	prickle
fish	school	rhinoceros	crash
frog	army	shark	shiver
giraffe	tower	squirrel	scurry
goose	gaggle	tiger	streak
gorilla	band		

3. When you've completed several cards, cut each one apart in a jigsaw pattern to divide the words. You can then mix up all the pieces and challenge children to match animals and groups, using the jigsaw pattern for help. Use removable wall adhesive to create a portable word wall with the cards. Children can take down the cards to explore, then match them up as they return them to the wall.

Awesome Animal Alliteration

Introduce a literary device as you build an animal alphabet!

1. To begin, work with children to brainstorm animals whose names begin with different letters of the alphabet. To keep your list organized, create a three-column chart on a sheet of chart paper. Write the letters of the alphabet down the first column. Leave the second column blank for now. Then write an animal in the third column, one for each letter (*alligator, bear, cat, duck, elephant, frog, giraffe, horse, iguana,* and so on).

2. Next, introduce the concept of alliteration by pointing out the first letter and sound of your "a" animal. Ask, "What is a word that describes this animal and begins with the same letter and sound?" Examples might include *angry alligator* or *amazing ant*. Write the adjective in the second column.

3. Continue down the list, creating alliterations such as *big bear, curious cat,* and *downy duck*.

4. When the list is complete, assign each child a letter and have children draw a picture of their animal, labeling it with the letter and the alliterative phrase. You can use the pictures to create an alphabet frieze for the classroom, or bind them together into a class alphabet book.

Whose Baby?

Create a matching game with animal baby names.

1. Begin by brainstorming a list of animal baby names with children. Ask: "What is a baby cat called?" (*kitten*) "How about a baby cow?" (*calf*) Continue with other familiar animals and babies, such as *duck/duckling, pig/piglet, sheep/lamb, bear/cub,* and *deer/fawn*. List each word pair on the board or chart paper.

2. Next, introduce children to some animal-baby word pairs that may be new to them, such as *goose/gosling, kangaroo/joey, mouse/pinkie, platypus/puggle,* and *swan/cygnet*.

3. Have children work with partners. Give each pair of children two index cards. Invite one child to draw and label the adult animal, and the other to draw and label its baby.

4. Collect all the cards into a deck and invite pairs of children to take turns playing Concentration. Players can place all the cards facedown in a grid and then take turns turning over two at a time. If the cards match, the player keeps the pair. If not, the cards get turned back over. Play continues until each animal has been matched with its baby.

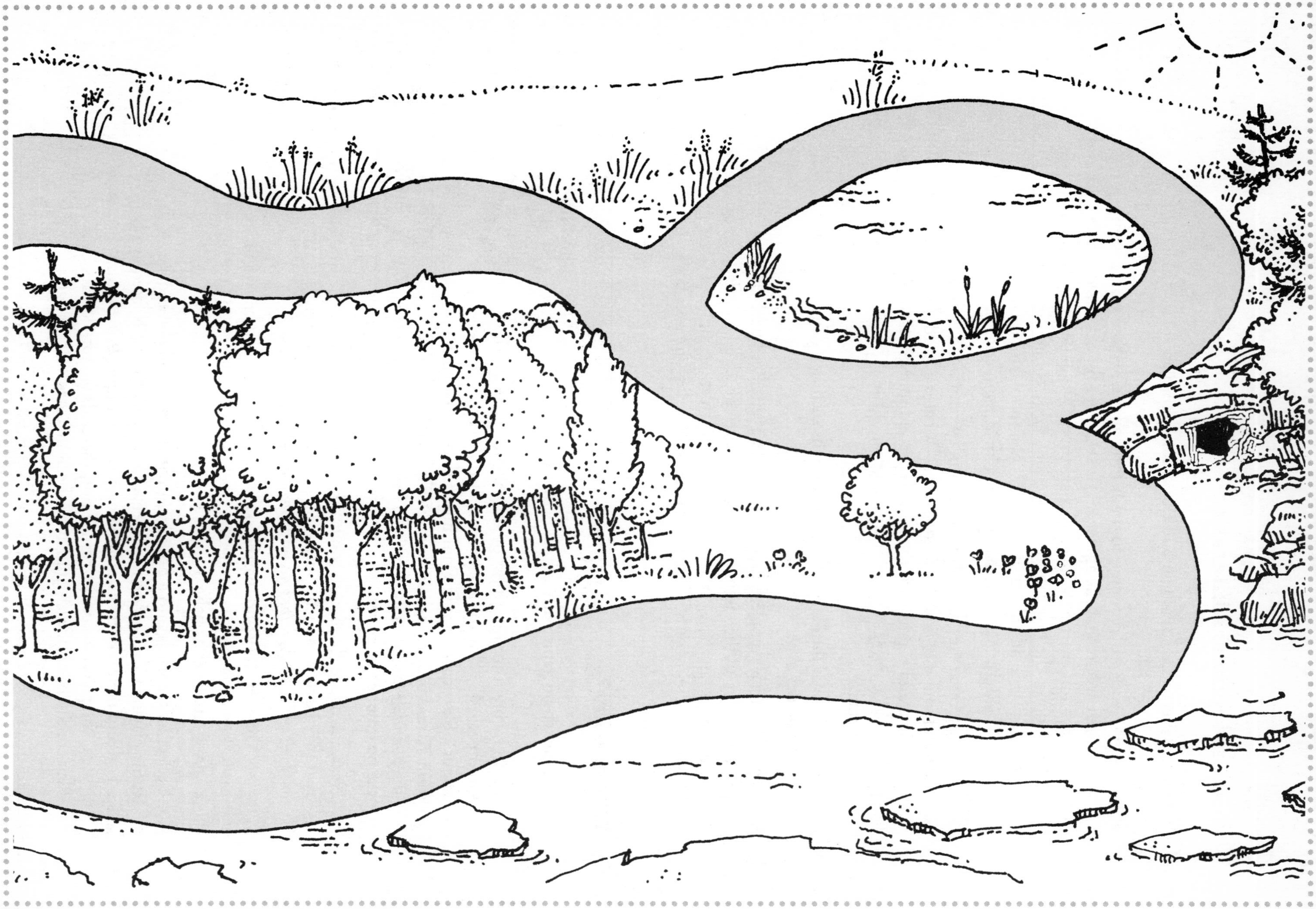

I went to the zoo

and I followed this track.

Then I looked at the _____

and the _____ looked back!

Weather and Seasons

There's no doubt about it—weather is one of the hottest topics of conversation around! Whether it's hot, cold, stormy, sunny, snowy, cloudy, or windy, the weather always gives people something to talk about. And since children learn from the world around them, it's a great subject to study. Most children are quite familiar with everyday words to describe weather, such as *hot, cold, snow, rain,* and *clouds.* But the character of the weather each day is far more nuanced than this—and ripe for building more subtle, sophisticated vocabulary. When children say it's "cold" outside, discuss the degree of coldness: is it merely *chilly,* or is it *freezing?* If it's "hot" outside, is it *balmy* or *warm* or *sticky?* In addition to descriptive words, the seasons provide a great opportunity to learn specific nouns. For instance, when it's winter, children might need to wear a *parka* or a *muffler.* In summer, they might need a *sunhat* or a *visor.*

A Word for All Seasons

Word walls are fabulous teaching tools because there's so much you can do with them! Word walls can inspire children's writing, become a basis for word-hunt and matching games, and also serve as spelling reminders. Using the patterns on page 70, you can create a word wall during each season—or do all four seasons at once!

Autumn	Winter	Spring	Summer
leaves	snow	flower	sunshine
rake	icicle	bloom	shorts
harvest	sled	rainy	sandals
apple	ice skates	umbrella	beach
pumpkin	frost	puddles	watermelon
squirrel	sweater	rainbow	sprinkler
acorn	scarf	grow	sweltering
chilly	gloves	sprout	ocean
windy	blizzard	robin	swimsuit
scarecrow	freezing	butterfly	mosquito

1. Make multiple copies of the patterns and cut out the symbols. For more durable word wall pieces, you can copy the patterns onto card stock. To add color, you can copy them directly onto colored paper. (Use lighter colors so the words will be easy to read.) If you choose to create one word wall at a time, set the other symbols aside for later use. If you choose to create a four-seasons wall, you can divide a bulletin board into four sections, placing one type of symbol in each.

2. Now it's time to start banking words! With children, brainstorm words that describe each season's weather in your area, special activities children do in each season, clothing children wear during each season, and so on. You can also add words at any time. If you discuss and record the daily weather during calendar time, add the words you use each morning. You might also get ideas by watching the forecast on television or reading the weather report in your local paper. Write each word on the appropriate seasonal pattern and attach it to the wall. Use the lists (page 66) to get started, and get children ready for a whole year of wonderful words!

Wish You Were Here!

Invite children to take an imaginary trip and write about the weather to the folks back home!

1. Create a postcard template by folding an $8\frac{1}{2}$ - x 11-inch sheet of paper in half to make an $8\frac{1}{2}$ - x $5\frac{1}{2}$ -inch rectangle. Then unfold the paper and draw a horizontal line on the crease. On the lower half of the paper, create a cloze postcard message with blanks for children to fill in. You can use the sample message at right, or create your own.

> Note: Fold top half back and glue backs together.
>
> Dear _____ ,
>
> Here I am in _____! It is _____ now, so the weather is _____.
> The trees look _____. I have been wearing _____ every day. I like the weather because I can _____!
>
> Love,
> _____.

2. Copy a class set of the postcard template and give one to each child. Have children fold the paper on the line and paste the backs together to create a front and a back. Now it's time to go on vacation! Invite children to think of a place they might go, and what season they might go in. (Children can also choose to "send" the postcard from your own area, and simply write about a particular season in your town.)

3. Have children write the name of the place on the first line and the season on the second. They can fill in the rest of the card by writing words to describe the weather (*sunny but cool, hot and sticky, stormy and wet*), how the trees look (*leafy, bare*), what they are wearing (*swimsuit, mittens*), and an activity appropriate to the weather and season (*swim, ski, jump in leaves*).

4. When children finish writing, have them turn their postcards over and draw a picture of the place they traveled to. Then let children "send" their postcards back and forth to their classmates.

Lost and Found

Hats, scarves, socks, and mittens—these items are important in dressing for the weather, but what child hasn't lost one? Create a "Lost and Found" bin that helps children build descriptive vocabulary.

1. Give each child a copy of the Lost and Found activity sheet (page 71). Have children cut out the clothing cards. Provide children with crayons and markers and invite them to choose one article of clothing to decorate. You might also provide collage materials such as fabric scraps, ribbon, and rickrack.

2. When children have decorated their item, invite them to create a "Lost" poster for it. They can write the name of the item at the top of the sheet of paper and then write or dictate a description including colors, patterns, and textures. Encourage children to come up with specific, interesting words, such as *crimson, aqua, downy,* and *velvety.*

3. Then have children glue their papers to the top half of a larger sheet of construction paper. (Children can decorate more items of clothing and create additional posters if they wish.)

4. When children are finished, collect all the clothing cards that children have colored, attach a piece of removable adhesive to the back of each one, and place them in a shoebox to create a "Lost and Found" bin. Display the posters on the walls of the classroom.

5. Now it's time to return the clothes to their owners! Invite children to choose an item from the bin and then read the posters on display. When they find the description that matches, they can attach the clothing to the bottom section of the poster. When each item has been matched, place all the clothing cards back in the bin and play again.

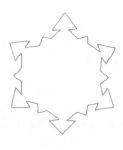

Compounding the Weather

Use weather and seasons to build and practice compound words.

Compound Seasonal and Weather Words	
iceberg	snowflake
icecap	snowshoe
rainbow	snowstorm
raincheck	snowsuit
raincoat	sunbeam
raindrop	sunburn
rainfall	sunflower
rainout	sunglasses
rainstorm	sunhat
snowball	sunlight
snowbound	sunscreen
snowfall	sunshine

1. First, introduce the concept of compound words by writing the word *raincoat* on chart paper. Ask, "What two smaller words can you find in this big word?" (*rain, coat*) Explain that when two words are joined together to make one word, it's called a compound word.

2. Brainstorm with children other compound words that can be formed with the word *rain*, such as *rainstorm*, *raindrop*, and *rainbow*. For each word, write the two smaller words on separate index cards.

3. Continue forming compound words that contain other seasonal and weather-related words, such as *snow, fall, sun, ice,* and *storm* (see the list, right, for ideas). Again, write the two small words that make up each compound word on separate index cards.

4. When you have a full deck of cards, create an interactive display by posting the words in two columns on a bulletin board or wall, in mixed-up order. Use the words for a variety of activities.

- Have children create compounds by re-sorting the columns.

- For a center-time game, pairs of children can use the cards to play "Compound Concentration." They place the cards facedown, then take turns turning over two at a time. If the two words can form a compound, the child keeps the cards. If not, they get turned back over. Play continues until no more compounds can be made.

- To incorporate a word-building element into any partner activity, place the cards in a paper bag, have each child select one at random, and have children attach the card to their shirt (for example, using a piece of double-sided tape). Children can then move about the classroom, looking for a child they can form a compound word with. Those children then become activity partners.

A Word for All Seasons

Word Wall Patterns

Lost!

One _____

Description:

_____

_____

_____

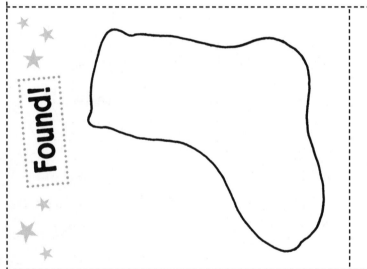

Found!

Found!

Found!

Found!

Holidays and Celebrations

Celebrations are times to express the joy that's inside all of us, and what better way to express it than with fun, magical holiday words. We need words to spin a spooky yarn come Halloween time, and words to tell our friends and family what we're thankful for on Thanksgiving. We need words to express the fulfillment that comes with giving to others over the winter holidays and words to tell loved ones how much we care on Valentine's Day. Holidays provide a special opportunity to teach children word relationships—how words can be grouped together to relate to a particular theme or idea. For example, the words *spider*, *bat*, *pumpkin*, *costume*, and *jack-o'-lantern* all remind people of Halloween. So each time you celebrate a holiday in your classroom, be sure to give children a second reason to be joyous: celebrate their growing word power!

Halloween Word Web

Reinforce word relationships by inviting children to spin a web of words!

1. Model how to create a word web: Draw a circle on chart paper, and then draw six spokes coming out from the circle. Write the word *Halloween* in the center circle. Ask, "What are some things that make you think of Halloween?" Write suggestions at the end of each spoke.

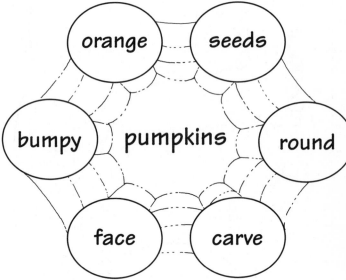

2. Give each child a copy of the Halloween Word Web (page 76; enlarge first, if desired). Have children choose a Halloween word to write in the center of the web, and then write a related word on each spider. To get them started, you might post a list of suggestions for the center word, such as *spiders*, *bats*, and *pumpkins*. To come up with related words, encourage children to consider what they know about the word in the center.

3. Post children's webs on a bulletin board as a reference for spooky holiday stories and poems.

Harvest Basket of Words

Children categorize words and concepts as they fill harvest baskets.

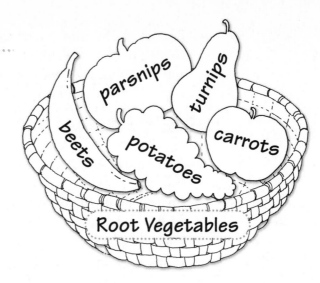

1. Make multiple copies of the harvest patterns (page 77–78). Cut out the basket, fruit, and vegetable shapes. On each basket, write a category related to the word *harvest*—for example, *Crops, Apples, Pumpkins, Root Vegetables,* and *Autumn*. Post each basket on a bulletin board.

2. Brainstorm words that go with each category. For instance, to go with "Apples," children might suggest the words *fruit, orchard, trees, crunchy, tart, sweet, cider, applesauce,* and *pie.*

3. Divide the class into small groups, one for each word category, and divide the fruit and vegetable shapes among groups. Invite children to work together to come up with words for their category and write them on the fruits and vegetables. Children can also color their food shapes if they wish; just remind them to make sure their words remain visible.

4. When children are finished, provide removable wall adhesive and let children take turns using their words to fill up the corresponding baskets. Read the words together. Later, remove the words and place them in a basket. Children can work independently or in pairs to re-sort the words into the baskets.

Teaching Tip

▲ ▲ ▲ ▲ ▲ ▲

As a variation, try a cornucopia of Thanksgiving words. Cut out large cornucopia shapes. Label the cornucopias with Thanksgiving-related categories, such as *Types of Pie* and *Things We Are Thankful For*. Write words on the fruit and vegetable patterns (page 78). Have children sort them into the cornucopias.

Gingerbread Rhymes

Word families—words that rhyme and end with the same spelling pattern—are a great way to build vocabulary.

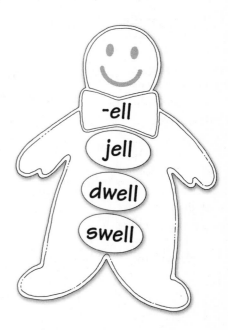

1. Enlarge and make multiple copies of the gingerbread and button patterns (page 79). Have children cut out and color the shapes. Write target phonograms on the bow ties—for example, *-ing, -ee, -ar,* and *-ight*. Attach the gingerbread patterns to a bulletin board.

2. Brainstorm three words for each phonogram—for example, *-ing* words might include *king, ring, thing,* and *swing*. (Introduce more sophisticated vocabulary such as *fling, cling,* and *wring* as children are ready.) Write each word on a button.

(continued)

3. Place all the buttons in a paper bag. Invite children to take turns coming up to the board, selecting a button, and attaching it to the appropriate gingerbread pattern (with removable wall adhesive).

Guess My Gift

Build descriptive vocabulary as you celebrate the spirit of giving!

1. Invite children to help you decorate an empty shoebox to look like a present. You can use wrapping paper to cover both the bottom and the lid, and add a bow to the lid.

2. Gather several "presents" to put in the box (any classroom item that can evoke descriptions, such as a favorite book or a box of crayons).

3. Seat children in a circle and select one volunteer to sit in the center. Have that child close his or her eyes as you silently show the present to the group and then place it in the gift box. Place the lid on the box, and have the child open his or her eyes.

4. Go around the circle, having each child say one word or phrase that describes what's in the box. For instance, a pencil might be described as "pointy," "long," "thin," "yellow," and "pink on one end." When each child has had a chance to share a description, have the child in the center guess the contents, then lift off the lid to check the guess. Choose a new volunteer and a new present, and play again.

Teaching Tip

▲▲▲▲▲▲▲

Use the blank heart pattern to create new word puzzles. You can have children match antonyms (*agree/disagree, immense/minute*), synonyms (*sad/forlorn, laugh/chuckle*), homophones (*pear/pair, sale/sail*), or rhymes (*pretty/city, laugh/calf*). You can even write a word on one side and a short definition on the other. Place the puzzle pieces in zip-close bags and provide them as an option for choice time.

Broken Heart Word Puzzles

These "broken hearts" teach compound words and word parts.

1. Copy and cut out several heart patterns (page 80), leaving each heart intact. Point out the word on the left side of the hearts. Explain that each of these words is often used on Valentine's Day. Explain that while each is a word on its own, it can also be part of a bigger word. By adding a new ending, the word changes. By adding another word, the word becomes a compound word (two words joined together to make a new word).

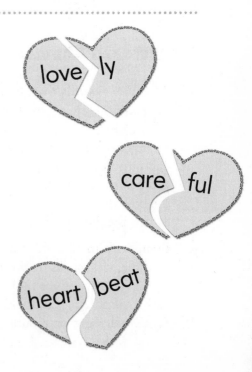

2. Brainstorm words that start with *heart, love,* and *care* (see samples, below). As you come up with words, write each word ending on the right side of the corresponding heart.

3. Cut apart the hearts on the jagged line. Then mix up all the pieces and challenge children to put the "broken words" back together again.

Heart Words	*Love* Words	*Care* Words
heartache	loveable	caring
heartbeat	lovebird	careful
heartbreak	loveless	carefree
heartfelt	lovely	careless
heartless	loveseat	caregiver
heartland	lovesick	caretaker
heartwarming	lovelorn	careworn

100th Day of School Big Book

Students build a collaborative book of 100 words.

1. Play "Categories" as you create a class Big Book. First, post ten sheets of chart paper on the walls of the classroom. Then take a vote to decide on ten categories for the game—for example, *Fruits, Vegetables, Animals, Book Genres, School Supplies, Sports, Musical Instruments, Outer Space, Vehicles,* and *Weather.* Write a category at the top of each sheet of chart paper, and then write the numerals 1 to 10 down the left side.

2. Give each child a marker and let children go around the room, adding words to the various lists. To avoid repetitions encourage children to read all previous words before adding to the list.

3. When each list has ten words, put the ten sheets together. Add a cover and title, then read your 100 words aloud to celebrate the 100th day of school!

Teaching Tip

▲▲▲▲▲▲

As an extension, plan a scavenger hunt for the days leading up to the 100th day of school. Give children large sheets of construction paper. Invite children to page through old magazines and newspapers and look for words they recognize—that is, words they can read and know the meanings of. Have them cut out these words and glue them on their paper. Their goal is to collect 100 words by the 100th day! Display children's word collages around the classroom. They will likely be filled with fun fonts and different colors, making them not only a source of pride, but also an inviting display.

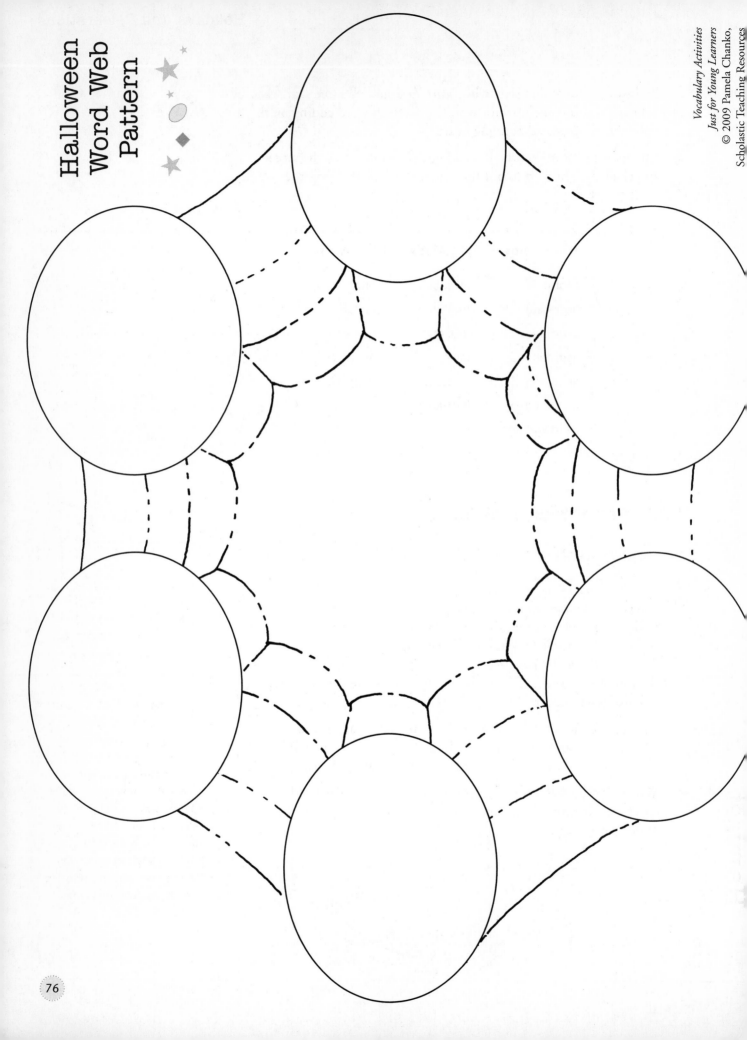

*Vocabulary Activities
Just for Young Learners*
© 2009 Pamela Chanko,
Scholastic Teaching Resources

Harvest
Basket of Words

Basket Pattern

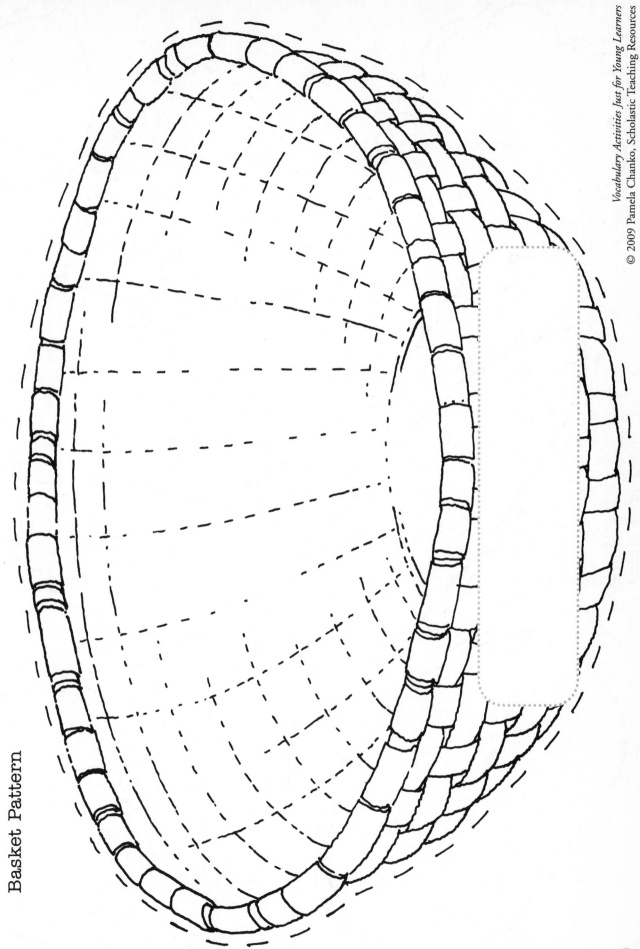

Vocabulary Activities Just for Young Learners, © 2009 Pamela Chanko, Scholastic Teaching Resources

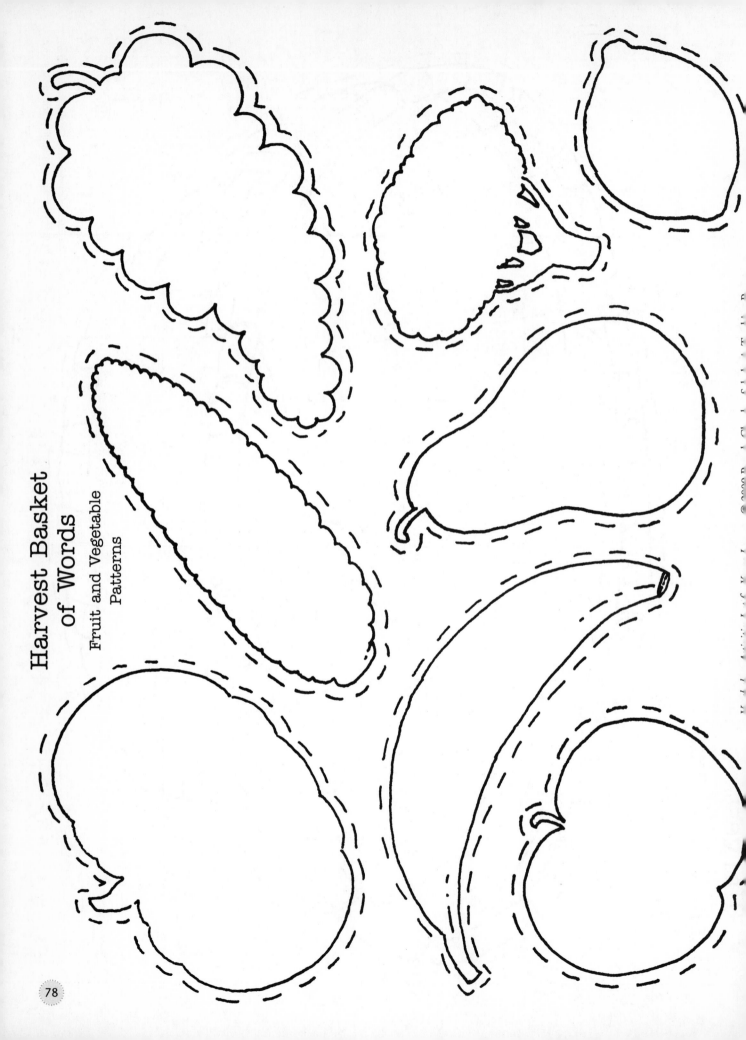

Harvest Basket
of Words

Fruit and Vegetable
Patterns

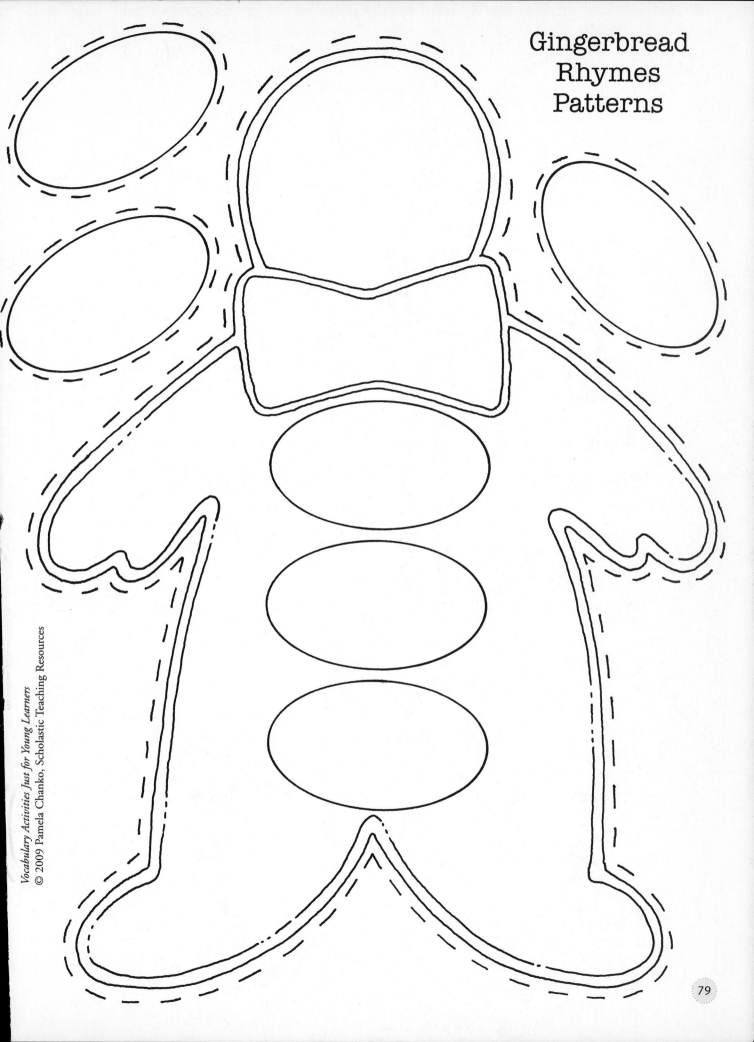

Gingerbread
Rhymes
Patterns

79

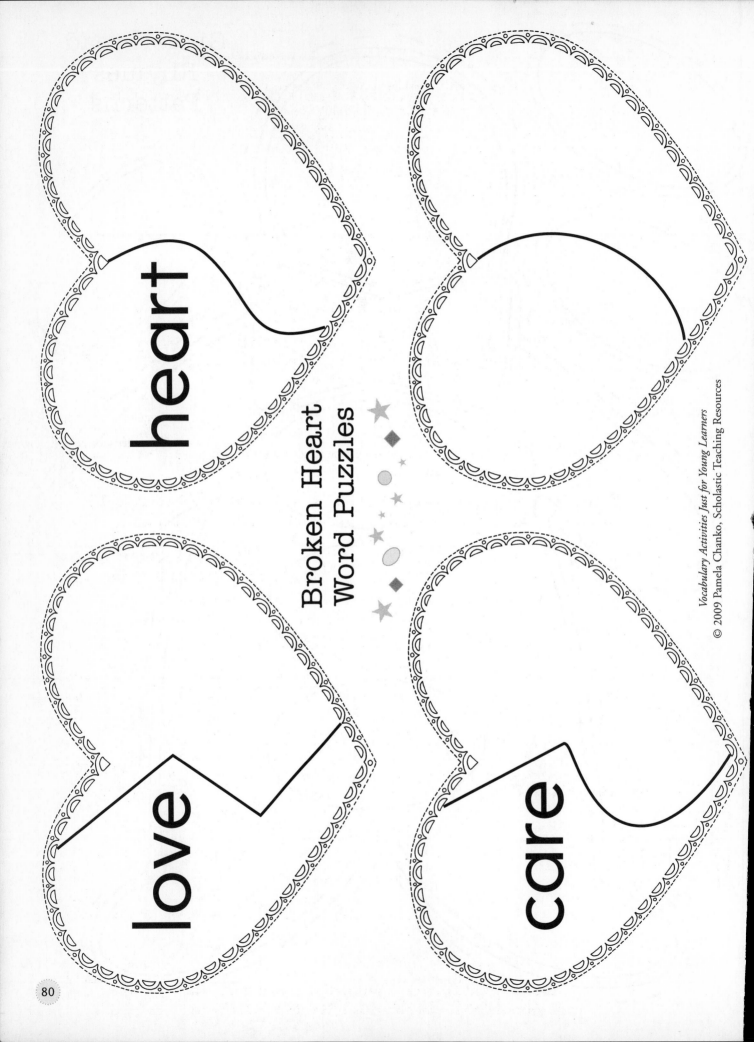

heart

love

care

**Broken Heart
Word Puzzles**